D1499194

Paulo Freire on Higher Education

SUNY Series, Teacher Empowerment and School Reform

Henry A. Giroux and Peter L. McLaren, Editors

Paulo Freire on Higher Education

A Dialogue at the National University of Mexico

Miguel Escobar, Alfredo L. Fernández, and Gilberto Guevara-Niebla with Paulo Freire

Foreword by Peter L. McLaren

Introduction by Carlos Alberto Torres

Afterword by Colin Lankshear

State University of New York Press

Published by
State University of New York Press, Albany

Printed in the United States of America

For information, address State University of New York Press,
State University Plaza, Albany, N.Y. 12246

Production by M. R. Mulholland
Marketing by Nancy Farrell

Library of Congress Cataloging-in-Publication Data

Escobar, Miguel, 1946–
    Paulo Freire on higher education : a dialogue at the National
University of Mexico / Miguel Escobar, Alfredo L. Fernándes,
and Gilberto Guevara-Niebla with Paulo Freire ; foreword by
Peter L. McLaren ; afterword by Colin Lankshear.
        p. cm. — (SUNY series, Teacher empowerment and school
reform)
    Proceedings of a seminar held at the National University of
Mexico.
    Includes bibliographical references (p.   ).
    ISBN 0-7914-1873-1 (cloth). — ISBN 0-7914-1874-X (pbk.)
    1. Education, Higher—Philosophy—Congresses. 2. Popular
education—Congresses. 3. Critical pedagogy—Congresses.
4. Freire, Paulo, 1921–   . I. Fernández, Alfredo L. II. Guevara-
Niebla, Gilberto, 1944–   . III. Freire, Paulo, 1921–   .
IV. Title. V. Series: Teacher empowerment and school reform.
LB2322.2.E83   1994
378'.001—dc20   93-15732
                                                          CIP
                                                          Rev.

Contents

Participants

Antonia Camarena, Professor, Faculty of Social and Political Sciences, UNAM.

Miguel Escobar, Professor, Faculty of Literature and Philosophy, UNAM.

Alfredo L. Fernández, Professor, Faculty of Literature and Philosophy, UNAM.

Paulo Freire, A well-known universal educator.

Raquel Glazman, Professor, Faculty of Literature and Philosophy, UNAM.

Gilberto Guevara-Niebla, Professor, Faculty of Literature and Philosophy, UNAM; Division of Humanities and Social Sciences, UAM (Xochimilco campus).

Fernando Jiménez Mier y Terán, Professor, Faculty of Social and Political Sciences, UNAM.

Ignacio Marbán, Professor, Faculty of Social and Political Sciences, UNAM.

Elías Margolis, Professor, Faculty of Social and Political Sciences, UNAM.

Eliezer Morales Aragón, Professor, Faculty of Economics, UNAM.

Faustino Ortega, Planning official, Division for University Planning, UNAM.

José Angel Pescador O., Professor, Faculty of Literature and Philosophy, UNAM.

Emilio Ribes, Professor, Department of Psychology, UNAM (Iztacala campus).

Blanca E. Solares, Professor, Faculty of Social and Political Sciences, UNAM.

Guillermo Villaseñor, Professor, Division of Humanities and Social Sciences, UAM (Xochimilco campus).

Felipe Rueda, Professor, Faculty of Social and Political Sciences, UNAM.

Foreword

I suggest those who have not read Amilcar Cabral's works on the struggle in Guinea Bissau take up the task of reviewing them. I am much impressed by his works, as well as those of Che Guevara. Furthermore, both shared a mutual respect for the other. It was in Guinea Bissau where the two met for the first time. They kept silence, observing one another. I would call it a revolutionary love with clasped hands (even though Amilcar was short and Guevara was an extraordinary specimen of a man). They both shared a love based on the revolution. And what was most interesting of all, they did many similar things— like being eminent pedagogues, great educators of the revolution.

Paulo Freire
Paulo Freire on Higher Education

It is a shame—since our North American cousins have unspeakable interests in this regards—that we continue to live in Latin America without knowing each other.

—Paulo Freire
Paulo Freire on Higher Education

I myself was a university professor for a long time, long before the coup in Brasil. But the professor I have become is not the professor I was. It couldn't be! It would be horrible! Even exile played an important part in my reeducation. It taught me that radicalization is a fundamental course and enabled me to go through different experiences as a university professor in different parts of the world: in Latin America, in the United States, in Canada, in Europe, in Africa, and in Asia.

—Paulo Freire
Paulo Freire on Higher Education

I remember in 1968 young people rebelled all around the world without coordinating themselves. Students in Mexico in 1968 were not telephoning young people in Harvard, or Columbia, or Prague, or Brazil. Nevertheless they carried out more or less the same movement. It was impressive. I also remember that communication between world universities was non-existent, and it was unbelievably easy for dominant classes to repress world wide movements.

—Paulo Freire
Paulo Freire on Higher Education

Educators and cultural workers in the United States live in the twilight of a crisis of democracy. The democratic aspiration of U.S. schooling and social, cultural, and institutional practices in general has been carried forth to an unheralded present moment in what retrospectively appears to have been an act of bad faith. The consequences of such an act for future generations are only faintly visible and are bathed in an ethos eerily reminiscent of earlier swindles of hope. Private enterprise, wage labor, free trade and other fundamental axes for the new capitalist world system have shrouded individuals in a web of promotional logic patterned by the conquering dynamism of Eurocentrism.

Capitalism carries the seeds of its own vulnerability and frailty even though its cunning appears inexhaustible. It's vulnerability is, ironically, the most steadfast and dangerous precondition for its further development. So long as it has bourgeois universal reason and the epistemic privilege of science as its spokesperson and Eurocentrism as its cultural anchor, its very constitution as a discourse of power needs to be challenged by popular movement of renewal within a polycentric cultural milieu.

Against the backdrop of the global underclass and the struggle for democracy exists the work of Paulo Freire, one of the great revolutionaries of our generation. It is important to make clear that Freire's work cannot be articulated outside the diverse and conflicting registers of indigenist cultural, intellectual, and ideological production in the Third World. *Third World* is a term that I use most advisedly after Benita Parry and Frantz Fanon to mean a "self-chosen phrase to designate a force independent of both capitalism and actually existing socialism, while remaining committed to socialist goals."[1] As such, it offers a starting point for a critique of imperialism and "retains its radical edge for interrogating the Western chronicle."

Of course, one of the powerful implications surrounding the distinction between First and Third Worlds involves the politics of underdevelopment. Andrew Ross describes the classic model of underdevelopment as one that benefits the small, indigenous elites of Western developed nations. Foreign markets such as those in Latin America provide a consumption outlet for the developed nations of the First World for absorbing the effects of a crisis of overproduction in the core economy. According to Ross, the peripheral economy (Latin America) underproduces for its domestic population. He reports that "The economic surplus which results from peripheral consumption of core products is appropriated either by core companies or by the domestic elites; it is not invested in the domestic economy of the peripheral nation."[2] Of course, what happens as a result is that the domestic economies of Latin America fail to possess the productive capacity to satisfy the most basic needs of most of the population. This is because "the only active sector is the one that produces commodities either for the indigeous elite or exotic staples for the core, metropolitan market."[3] The contact between Latin America and foreign capital certainly does encourage peripheral economies to develop, but such development—if you can call it that— is almost always uneven; consequently, such contact forces the peripheral economy to underdevelop its own domestic spheres.

When there is economic dependency, cultural dependency often follows in its wake. However the capitalist culture industry is not simply superstructural but constitutive in that the masses—in both First and Third Worlds—do not simply consume culture passively as mindless dupes. There is often resistance at the level of symbolic meaning that prevents the culture industry from serving simply as a vehicle of repressive homogenization of meaning. According to Ross, the elites of the peripheral nations are the first to acquire access to Westernized popular culture, because of the limited access of the indigenous population to the media, the media generally serve to encourage affluent groups to adopt the consumer values of the most developed countries.[4] The elites basically serve in a supervisory capacity when it comes to the cultural consumption of the indigenous peasantry. However, the continuing ties of the peasantry to their own ethnic cultures does help them become less dependent on Western information. Foreign mass-produced culture is often interpreted and resisted at the level of popular culture, and we must remember that First World cultural values can also be affected by its contact with the cultures of less developed countries. And, further, not everything about contact with Western culture is to be shunned. For instance, my own contact with Brasilian feminists has revealed to my that oppositional feminist critique in the U.S. can be successfully appropriated by Brasilian women in their struggle against the structures of patriarchal oppression, structures can permit men to kill their wives if they suspect them of infidelity—on the grounds that their "male honor" has been violated.

The image of Freire that is evoked against this recurring narrative of the decline and deceit of Western democracy and the cultural hegemony of developed nations is a distant voice in a crowd, that of a disturbing interloper among the privileged and powerful—one who bravely announces that the emperor has no clothes. Ethically and politically Freire remains haunted by the ghosts of history's victims and possessed by the spirits that populate the broken dreams of utopian thinkers and millenarian dreamers—a man whose capacities for nurturing affinities between disparate social, cultural, and political groups and for forging a trajectory towards moral, social and political liberation exceeds the disasters that currently befall this world.

Freire's internationally celebrated praxis began in the late 1940s and continued unabated until 1964, when he was arrested in Brazil as a result of a literacy program he designed and implemented in 1962. He was imprisoned by the military government for sevety days and exiled for his work in the national literacy campaign, of which he had served as director. Freire's sixteen years of exile were tumultuous and productive times: he spent five years in Chile as a UNESCO consultant with the Chilean Agrarian Reform Corporation, specifically the

Reform Training and Research Institute; was appointed in 1969 to Harvard University's Center for Studies in Development and Social Change; moved to Geneva, Switzerland, in 1970 as consultant to the Office of Education of the World Council of Churches, where he developed literacy programs for Tanzania and Guinea-Bissau that focused on the re-Africanization of their countries; developed literacy programs in some postrevolutionary former Portuguese colonies such as Angola and Mozambique; assisted the governments of Peru and Nicaragua with their literacy campaigns; established the Institute of Cultural Action in Geneva in 1971; briefly returned to Chile after Salvador Allende was assassinated in 1973; provoked General Pinochet to declare Freire a subversive; and eventually return to Brazil in 1980 to teach at the Pontificia Universidade Católica de São Paulo and the Universidade de Católica de São Paulo and the Universidade de Campinas in São Paulo. During this period he also produced numerous works, most notably *Pedagogy of the Oppressed, Cultural Action for Freedom,* and *Pedagogy in Process: Letters to Guinea-Bissau.*

Little did Freire realize that on November 15, 1988 the *Partido dos Trabalhadores* (Workers Party of PT) would win the municipal elections in São Paulo, Brazil, and be appointed secretary of education of the city of São Paulo by Mayor Luiza Erundina de Sousa. Relentlessly destabilizing as *sui generis* and autochthonous mercenary pedagogy—that is spontaneous pedagogy wantonly designed to stimulate the curiosity of students yet imposed in such a bourgeois manner so as to "save" those who live in situtations of domestication only whent hey are reinitiated into the conditions of their own oppression—Freire's praxias of solidarity, that is, his critical pedagogy, speaks to a new way of being and becoming human. This "way of being and becoming" constitutes a quest for the historical self-realization of the oppressed by the oppressed themselves through the formation of collective agents of insurgency. Against the treason of modern reason, Freire aligns the role of the educator with that of the organic intellectual. It should come as no surprise, then, that—against perspectives generated in the metropolitan epicenters of education designed to serve and protect the status quo—Freire's work has, even today, been selected for a special disapprobation by the lettered bourgeoise and epigones of apolitical pedagogy as a literature to be roundly condemned, travestied, traduced, and relegated to the margins of the education debate. That Freire's work has been placed under prohibition, having been judged to be politically inflammatory and subversive, is understandable given the current historical conjunction. But it is not inevitable.

It is not the purpose of this introduction to address the often egregious misrepresentations of Freire's work by mainstream educators, nor is it to simply situate Freire unproblematically within the context of First World efforts to ground liberation struggles in pedagogical practices. I intend merely to elaborate on one of the central themes of *Paulo Freire on Higher Education*, which is the role of the educator as an active agent of social change.

Critical Pedagogy versus the Academy

While their political strategies vary considerably, critical educators of various stripe (many of whom have been directly influenced by Freire's work) generally share certain presuppositions, which can be summarized as follows: pedagogies constitute a form of social and cultural criticism; all knowledge is fundamentally mediated by linguistic relations that inescapably are socially and historically constituted; individuals are synechochically related to the wider society through traditions of mediation (family, friends, religion, formal schooling, popular culture, etc.); social facts can never be isolated from the domain of values or removed from forms of ideological production as inscription; the relationship between concept and object and that between signifier and signified is neither inherently stable nor trans-cendentally fixed and is often mediated by circuits of capitalist production, consumption, and social relations; language is central to the formation of subjectivity (conscious and uncounscious awareness); certain groups in any society are unnecessarily and often unjustly privileged over other, and while the reason for this privileging may very widely, the oppression that charac-terizes contemporary societies is most forcefully secured when subordinates accept their social status as natural, necessary, inevitable, or bequeathed to them as an exercise of historical chance; oppression has many faces and focusing on only one at the expense of others (e.g., class oppression vs. racism) often elides or occults the interconnection among them; power and oppression cannot be understood simply in terms of an irrefutable calculus of meaning linked to cause-and-effect conditions, and this means that an unforseen world of social relations awaits us; domination and oppression are implicated in the radical contingency of social development and our responses to it; and mainstream research practices are generally and unwittingly implicated in the reproduction of systems of class, race, and gender oppression.[5]

　　Freire's work certainly reflects this list of assumptions to different degrees; and while his corpus of writing does not easily fall under the rubric of poststructuralism, his emphasis on the relationship among language, experience, power, and identity certainly give weight to certain poststructuralist assumptions. For instance, Freire's work stresses that language practices among individuals and groups do more than reflect reality: they effectively organize our social universe and reinforce what is considered to be the limits of the possible while constructing at the same time the faultlines of the practical. To a large extent, the sign systems and semiotic codes that we use are always already populated by prior interpretations, since they have been necessarily conditioned by the material, historical, and social formations that help to give rise to them. They endorse and enforce particular social arrangements, since they are situated in historically conditioned social practices in which the desires and motivations of certain groups have been culturally and ideologically inscribed, not to mention overdetermined. All sign systems are fundamentally arbitrary, but certain systems have been accorded a privileged distinction over other, in ways that bear the imprint of race, class, and gender struggles.[6] Sign systems not only are culture bound and onventional but also are distributed socially, historically, and geopolitically.[7] For U.S. educators, this implicates our language use in Euro-American social practices that have been forged in the crucible of patriarchy and white supremacy.

Knowledge does not, according to the view sketched above, possess any inherent meaningfulness in and of itself but depends on the context in which such knowledge is produced and the purpose to which such knowledge is put. If there is no preontological basis for meaning that is extralinguistically verifiable, no philosophical calculus that can assist us in making choices, then we can come to see language as a form of power that apprentices us to particular ways of seeing and engaging the self and others and this in turn, has particular social consequences and political effects.[9] Few educators have helped us to judge the political effects of language practices as much as Paulo Freire. And few educators have been as misused and misunderstood. Clearly, Freire does not see individuals and groups to be agentless beings invariably trapped in and immobilized by language effects. Rather, he sees human beings as *politically accountable* for their language practices, and, thus agency is considered immanent.[10] Freire's position reflects Gramsci's notion that the structural intentionality of human beings needs to be critically interrogated through a form of *conscientização* (conscientization; this Portuguese word is defined by Freire as a deep or critical reading of commonsense reality).

The University as (a) Moral Agent

When the surgical pick of Egas Moniz was poised to perform the first medical lobotomy (a procedure that, it may be recalled, won him the Nobel Prize and led reactionary advocates to consider lobotomies for individuals subversive of good citizenship practices), it was inconceivable to think that such an act of cerebral terrorism could be achieved at a cultural level more effectively and much less painfully through the powerful articulations of new and ever more insidious forms of capitalist hegemony. The emancipatory role of university and public intellectuals, as well as the function of the organic intellectual, has been greatly diminished by this process. In fact, emancipatory praxis has been largely orphaned in our institutions of education, as educators are either unable or refuse to name the political location of their own pedagogical praxis. Part of the problem is that postmodern traditions of mediation have become simulacra whose ideological dimensions cannot easily be identified with or organically linked to the most oppressive effects of capitalist social relations and material practices. The redoubled seduction of new information technologies not only rearticulates a submission to multinational financial strategies but also creates possibilities for a resignification of, resistance to, and popular participation in the politics of everday life. The fact that relationships between the specific and the general have become blurred by these new electronic forces of mediation has both increased a reorganization and liberation of difference and posed a danger of further cultural fragmentation and dissolution limiting the struggle for strategic convergences among sites of intellectual production, the formation of new moral economies, and the expansion of new social movements. This disaggregation of public spheres and the massification of *mestizaje* identities makes it difficult to establish the solidarities necessary for developing liberating idioms of social transformation.[11] It is to a deeper understanding of the relationship between the role of hegemony in the formation of university intellectuals and their students and the function of the university itself in the context of wider social and political formations that this book was created.

Recently Sande Cohen has offered a forceful challenge to the timid and frequently duplicitous role that university intellectuals have assumed in relation to the sociality of capital and the "catastrophe of socialized expectations." Following the persistent contentions of Baudrillard, Nietzsche, and other, Cohen maintains that objectivity can no longer hide or deny its subjectively based interests—a situation that has serious implications for the role of the intellectual in contemporary North American society. He writes:

> For intellectuals it is suggested that our texts and objects now fail to connect with everthing but *our own simulacra, image power, formation of exchange.* In doubting and negating everthing, in affirming and consecrating everything, intellectuals remain prisoners of the futile role of the subject-in-consciousness and enforce the pretense that our efforts *translate and represent* for the truth of others, the reality of the world.[12]

For Cohen, as for Freire, the dilemma of the intellectual lies in the failure to forcefully challenge the perils of capitalism. In response to this dilemma, Cohen mounts an articulate and vigorous attack on the U.S. professoriate. University discourse and practices are condemned as mobilizing the academicization and domestication of meaning through a modernist process of historicization—a process that, in effect, amounts to creating various self-serving theologies of the social that enable professors to speculate on the future in order to justify their social function as intellectuals. Resulting from this process are acute forms of antiskepticism leading in many instances to a debilitating cynicism. According to Cohan, universities and their academic gentry operate as a discursive assemblage directed at creating a regime of truth, a process that fails to undertake the important task of "inventing systems independent of the system of capital."[13] In this instance, academic criticism is crippled by its inability to break from conventional catagories such as "resemblance." Critical languages forged in the theoretical ovens of the academy simply and regrettably pursue their own hegemony through the production of pretense and the desire for power. Further, in face of the cultural logic of late capitalism, "the category of the intellectual is disengaged from any possible antimodernist argument."[14] This situation recenters "high status" knowledge within the liberal tradition of therapeutic discourse. According to Cohen, "Universities cannot speak to their own participation in the destruction of events without undoing their 'need' and control structure."[15]

Even Habermas's now popular appeal for a rational means of resolving differences and restoring democratic social life in the ideal speech situation is described as "psychologically based moral economy"[16] in which "intellectuals are empowered so long as they stay in the precut grooves of providing resocialization with concepts, theory, sophistication, the seductions, one might say, of bureaucratic integration."[17] With this dilemma in mind, Cohen asserts:

> Why isn't capitalism—which makes mincemeat of real argumentation by its homogenization of signifiers, accomplished, for example, by the media's ordinary excessive displacement of analysis or the marginalization of unfamiliear cultural and social voices—rendered more critically?. . .Why is the economic mode so accepted in the first place as an unalterable form of social relation? Why is criticism so often an opposition that acts under the identity of a "loyal opposition"?[18]

In order to escape the inevitability under capitalism of a modernist historicist recoding of knowledge, Cohen astutely adopts Lyotard's notion of 'dispossession'. Dispossession is recruited in this context in terms of "the dispossession of historicizing, narrating, reducing, demanding."[19] More specifically, it refers to a form of "uncontrolled presentation (which is not reducible to presence)."[20] It also points to the suspension of identification—including negative identification. Cohen also conscripts into the service of a critique of captialism Hannah Arendt's concept of "active critique" of ends and goals "that never identif[ies] with time valuations which are, unavoidably, always already atrophied."[21] We are advised here to "strangify," a term he employs in tandem with an unyielding commitment to resubjectification—to making subjectivity different outside the acts of negation and opposition through the creation of insubordinate signifiers that loosen and "neutralize . . . the Platonic control on the power to select."[22] To strangify is to engage in a nonreduction of meaning that terrorizes all forms of equational logic, positive and negative.[23]

Cohen's project of strangification—a type of postmodern extension of Freire's term of conscientization—is directed at destabilizing and decentering the monumentalization of the already known and the militarization of existing sign systems established by the academic gentry and mandarins of high-status knowledge whose participation is aimed at the legitimization of their own power. Along with smashing through the Western arcs of destiny—those supposedly unassailable narratives of individual freedom arching toward Disneyland or Gangsterland—strangification unsettles foundational myths that anchor meaning in a sedentary web of contradictory appearances and precode the world in such a way that entrance to the world of 'success' depends on the imprimatur of one's cultural captial and the potential for earning power.

The Nocturnal Academy and the Politics of Difference

Western intellectuals need to further understand that while affirming the experiences of subaltern groups is exceedingly important within a praxis of liberation, it is highly questionable to render the "other" as transparent by inviting the other to speak for herself. Freire and other critics make this point very clear. As Gaurav Desai (following Gayatri Spivak, Lata Mani, and Partha Chattergee) notes, the position of permitting the other to speak for herself is uncomfortably "complicitious with a Western epistemological tradition that takes the conditions of the possibility of subaltern counterinvention for granted without engaging in a critique of the effects of global capitalism on such counterinvention."[24] Since the oppressed speak for themselves within a particular sign structure, the language of critique adopted by the insurgent intellectual needs to be able to analyze the embeddedness of such a sign system in the larger episteme of colonialism and white supremacist, capitalist patriarchy. Insurgent intellectuals must apply the same critique to their won assumptions about the other as they do to the other's self-understanding. In fact, critical educators need to counterinvent a discourse that transcends existing epistemes.[25]

Jim Merod poses the challenge of the intellectual as follows:

The critic's task is not only to question truth in its present guises. It is to find ways of putting fragments of knowledge, partial views, and separate disciplines in contact with questions about the use of expert labor so that the world we live in can be seen for what it is.[26]

The problem, as Merod sees it, is that there exists within the North American academy no political base for alliances among radical social theorists and the oppressed. He writes:

> The belief among liberal humanists that they have no "liberation strategy" to direct their steps is a vivid reminder of the humanities' class origin. Yet intellectuals always have something to fight for more important than their own professional position. North American intellectuals need to move beyond theory, tactics, and great dignified moral sentiments to support, in the most cencrete ways possible, people harmed or endangered by the guiltless counterrevolutionary violence of state power... .The major intellectual task today is to build a political community where ideas can be argued and sent into the world of news and information as a force with a collective voice, a voice that names cultural distortions and the unused possibilities of human intelligence.[27]

One important task of the critical educator is to translate cultural difference. This is certainly the challenge for Freirian educators. The act of translation is, in Bhabha's (1990) cultural languages are to a certain extent foreign to themselves and from the perspective of otherness it is possible to interrogate the contextual specificity of cultural systems.[29] It is in this sense, then, that "it becomes possible to inscribe the specific locality of cultural systems—their incommensurable differences— and through that apprehension of difference, to perform the act of cultural translation."[30]

All forms of cultural meaning are open to translation, because all cultural meanings resist totalization and complete closure. In other words, cultural meanings are hybrid and cannot be contained within any discourse of authenticity or race, class, gender, essences. Bhabha describes the subject of cultural difference as follows:

> the subject of cultural difference is neither pluralistic nor relativistic. The frontiers of cultural difference are always belated or secondary in the sense that their hybridity is never simply a question of the admixture of pre-given identities or essences. Hybridity is the perplexity of the living as it interrupts the representation of the fullness of life; it is an instance of iteration, in the minority discourse, of the time of the arbitrary sign—"the minus in the origin"—through which all forms of cultural meaning are open to translation because their enunciation resists totalization.[31]

The subaltern voices of minority cultures constitue "those people who speak the encrypted discourse of the melancholic and the migrant."[32] The transfer of *their* meaning can never be total. The "desolate silences of the wandering people"[33] illustrates the incommensurability of translation that confronts the descourse of white supremacist and capitalist patriarchy with its own alterity.

As translators, critical educators must assume a transformative role by "dialogizing the other" rather than trying to "represent the other."[34] The site of translation is always an arena of struggle. The translation of other cultures must resist the authoritative representation of the other through a decentering process that challenges dialogues that have become institutionalized through the semantic authority of state power. Neither the practice of signification nor translation occurs in an ideological void, and for this reason educators need to interrogate the sign systems that are used to produce readings of experience. As Joan Scott notes: "experience is a subject's history. Language is the site of history's enactment."[35] It is Freire's particular strength that he has developed a critical vernacular that can help to translate both the other's experience and his own experience of the other in such a way that ideological representations may be challenged. The challenge here is to rethink authoriative representations of the other in a critical language that does not simply reauthorize the imperatives of First World translation practices. This would constitute a form of cultural imperialism. Experiences never speak for themselves, even those of the oppressed. Freire is careful to make sure his own language of translation provides the oppressed with tools to analyze their own experiences; at the same time he recongizes that the translation process itself is never immune from inscription in ideological relations of power and privilege.

While Freire's dialogue in this book does not centrally address the politics of race, his message can nonetheless be elaborated through an engagement with the work of black insurgent intellectuals. Cornel West blames what he perceives as a decline in black literate intellectual activity on the "relatively greater Black integration into postindustrial capitalist America with its bureaucratized, elite universities, dull middlebrow colleges, and decaying high schools, which have little concern for and confidence in Black students as potential intellectuals."[36] He is highly critical of "aspects of the exclusionary and repressive effects of White academic institutions and humanistic scholarship"[37] and, in particular, "the rampant xenophobia of bourgeois humanism predominant in the whole academy."[38] West sketches out four models for black intellectual activity as a means of enabling critical forms of black literate activity in the United States. The bourgeois humanist model is premised on black intellectuals possessing sufficient legitimacy and placement within the "hierarchial ranking and the deep-seated racism shot through bourgeois humanistc scholarship."[39] Such legitimation and placement must, however, "result in Black control over a portion of or significant participation within, the larger White infra-structures for intellectual activity."[40]

The Marxist revolutionary model, according to West, is "the least xenophobic White intellecutal subculture available to Black intellectuals."[41] However, West is also highly critical of the constraints Marxist discourse places on the creative life of black intellectuals in terms of constructing a project of possibility and hope, including an analytical apparatus to engage short-term public policies. According to West:

> the Marxist model yields Black-intellectual self–satisifaction which often inhibits growth; also highlights social structural constraints with little practical direction regarding conujunctural oppor-tunities. This self-satisfaction results in either dogmatic submission to and upward mobility with sectarian party or pre-party formations, or marginal placement in the bourgeois academy equipped with cantankerous Marxist rhetoric and sometimes insighful analysis utterly divorced from the integral dynamics, concrete realities, and progressive possi-bilities of the Black community. The preoccupation with social structural constraints tends to produce either preposterous chiliastic projections or paralyzing, pessimistic pronouncements.[42]

It is important to point out amidst all of this criticism that West does recognize the enabling aspects of the Marxist revolutionary model in its promotion of critical consciousness and its criticisms of dominant research programs within the bourgeois academy.

The Foucaultian postmodern skeptic model invoked by West investigates the relationship among knowledge, power, discourse, politics, cognition, and social control. It offers a fundamental rethinking of the role of the intellectual within the contemporary postmodern condition. Foucault's "political economy of truth" is viewed by West as a critique of both bourgeois humanist and Marxist approaches through the role of Foucault's specific intellectual. The specific intellectual, according to West

shuns the labels of scientificity, civility, and prophecy, and instead deves into the specificity of the political, economic, and cultural matrices within which regimes of truth are produced, distributed, circulated, and consumed. No longer should intellectuals deceive themselves by believing—as do humanist and Marxist intellectuals—that they are struggling "on behalf" of the truth; rather the problem is the struggle over the very status of truth and the vast institutional mechanism which account for this status.[43]

West summarizes the Foucaultian model as an encouragement of "an intense and incessant interrogation of power-laden discourses."[44] But the Foucaultian model is not a call to revolution. Rather, it's an invitation to revolt against the repressive effects of contemporary regimes of truth.

Selectively appropriating from these three models, West goes on to propose his own "insurgency model," which posits the black intellectual as a critical, organic catalyst for social justic. His insurgency model for black intellectual life recovers the emphasis on human will and heroic effort from the bourgeois model, highlights the emphasis on structural contraints, class formations, and radical democratic values from the Marxist model, and recuperates the worldy skepticism evidenced in the Foucaultian mode's destabilization of regimes of truth. However, unlike the bourgeois model, the insurgency model privileges collective intellectual work and communal resistance and struggle. Contrary to the Marxist model, the insurgency model does not privilege the industrial working class as the chosen agent of history but rather attacks a variety of forms of social hierarchy and subordination, both vertical and horizontal. Further, the insurgency model places much more emphasis on social conflict and struggle than does the Foucaultian model. While Freire's critique of domesticating forms of pedagogy gives a specifically Latin American context for the development of the insurgent intellectual, West's own typology extends some central Freirean themes in order to deepen its engagement with issues of race.

bell hooks describes an intellectual as "somebody who trades in ideas by transgressing discursive frontiers. . .who trades in ideas in their vital bearing on a wider political culture."[45] However, hooks argues that white supremacist capitalist patriarchy has denied black women, especially, "the opportunity to pursue a life of the mind." This is a problem that is also firmly entrenched in the racist white university system that involves "persecution by professors, peers, and professional collegues."[46] hooks rightly notes that "any discussion of intellectual work that does not underscore the conditions that make such work possible misrepresents the concrete circumstances that allow for intellectual production."[47] She further elaborates:

Within a White supremacist capitalist, patriarchal social context like this culture, no Black woman can become an intellectual without decolonizing her mind. Individual Black women may become successful academics without undergoing this process and, indeed, maintaining a colonized mind may enable them to excel in the academy but it does not enhance the intellectual process. The insurgency model that Cornal West advocates, appropriately identifies both the process Black females must engage to become intellectuals and the critical standpoints we must assume to sustain and nurture that choice.[48]

I have employed criticisms of the academy by West, hooks, and Cohen in this introduction because concerns dealing with postmodern social conditions and theory and those of race and gender help to widen Freire's discussion and those of his colleagues by situating their insights more fully within the context and concerns of North American liberation struggles, specifically as they address struggles of the poor, of women, and people of color. Of course, there is room to broaden the context even further in relation to the struggles of indigenous peoples, of gays and lesbians, and other cultural workers within and outside of university settings. Despite these absent discourses, *Paulo Freire on Higher Education* remains vitally important in the current debates over the role of the university in North America. Freire warns educators that the activity of reading the word in relation to the social world has been regrettably pragmatic rather than principled. In other words, schooling (in relation to both universities and public schools) revolves around the necessity of differentially reproducing a citizenry distinguished by class, race, and gender injustices. The challenges of educators in both First and Third World contexts is to transform these reproductive processes.

As a teacher, Freire has provided the pedagogical conditions necessary to understand that Enlightenment humanism and its specifically Eurocentric (and Euro-American) "voice of reason" has not always been insightful or even reasonable in exercising its transcontinental thinking in the service of truth and justice. *Paulo Freire on Higher Education* helps us to further confront this issue as well as many others of concern to educators and cultural workers.

Paulo Freire on Higher Education is a book that can help deepen the debate over the role of the university in contemporary North American culture and, by extension, can also help to situate the struggle of Latin American educators within the concerns of postmodern and insurgent criticisms of the academy as exemplified in the criticisms offered by West, hooks, and Cohen.

In a world of global capitalism we need global alliances though cultural and political contact in the form of critical dialogue. Samir Amin (1989) notes that we collectively face a problem that "resides in the objective necessity for a reform of the world system; failing this, the only way out is through the worst barbarity, the genocide of entire peoples or a worldwide conflagration."[49]

In attempting to develop a project premised on the construction of an emancipatory cultural imaginary that is directed at transforming the conditions that create the victims of capitalist expansion, educators need to go beyond simply severing their arterial connections to the forces of production and consumption that defraud them through the massification of their subjectivities. Rather, they need to create new alliances through a politics of difference. Otherwise, they face the prospect of becoming extensions of multinational corporations within the larger apparatus of capitalist expansion in the service of unequal accumulation and further underdevelopment in the peripheral and semiperipheral countries of Latin America.

We are reminded of Freire and his colleagues not to engage in controversies about difference but rather to be encouraged to dialogue about difference. It is in this sense that the university is invited to beome truly plural and dialogical, a place where studetns are required not only to read texts but to understand contexts. A place where educators are required to learn to talk about student experiences and then form this talk into a philosophy of learning and a praxis of transformation.

I have recently witnessed in Brasil an experiment using Freire's work in conjunction with contributions by critical educators in Europe and the United States at Escola 1.º e 2.º Graus José César de Mesquita. The project is currently supported by the Sindicato des Trabalhadores nas Indústrias Metalúrgicas Mecânicas e Material Eléctrico de Porto Alegre. Here, the curriculum has been forged out of dialogues among teacher, researchers, and scholars from many different countries in both First and Third Worlds. While there exists a great deal of political opposition to this school for workers (a public school and high school consisting of a thousand students who live in an industrial zone in Porto Alegre) from both reactionary and neoliberal educators, administrators, and politicians, the experiment itself is a testament to the Freirean vision of transcultural alliances and geopolitical realignment.

Critical pedagogy argues that pedagogical sites, whether they are universities, public schools, museums, art galleries, or other spaces, must have a vision that is not content with adapting individuals to a world of oppressive social relations but is dedicated to transforming the very conditions that promote such conditions. This means more than simply reconfiguring or collectively refashioning subjectivities outside of the compulsive ethics and consumerist ethos of flexible specialization or the homogenizing calculus of capitalist expansion. It means creating new forms of sociality, new idioms of transgression, and new instances of popular mobilization that can connect the institutional memory of the academy to the tendential forces of historical struggle and the dreams of liberation that one day might be possible to guide them. This is a mission that is not simply Freirean but immanently human.

Peter L. McLaren
Santa Maria
Rio Grande do Sul, Brasil

Preface

More than an academic work, this book is a testimony of the political and educational thought of a group of professors from the National University of Mexico (UNAM, Universidad Nocional Autonoma of Mexico) who took advantage of the opportunity to have Paulo Freire's pressence on their campus to build an educational discourse focused on his work and practice.

The UNAM professors were interested in having a dialogue with the well-known contemporary, humanistic educator Paulo Freire concerning three main problems in contemporary education: power and education, curriculum and social reality, and the role of intellectuals. Freire generously agreed to participate without an honorarium and the National University of Mexico supplied the elements required to organize a three-day seminar on the relationship between education and society.

Paulo Freire agreed that the main purpose of the seminar would be to take him as the intellectual stimulus for a three-day debate. Under this assumption, the seminar was planned in such as way that would produce a *"speaking book"* with a new contribution from Paulo Freire that would enlarge the knowledge about educational emancipation (self-reliance). The seminar was recorded and transcribed and the resulting drafts were fully revised by each one of the participants. We, the coordinators of the seminar, then edited the work to give it coherence and appeal. We chose appropriate subtitles to manifest the critical nature of the seminar discussions.

Finally, this work would not have been achieved without the strong support, in different ways, of Elena Sandoval, Carmen Carrion Carranza, and Rosy Romero.

We hope that this book will be very interesting for those engaged in the theory and practice of critical education. The full responsibility for the structure of this work is ours.

M. Escobar, A. L. Fernández, and G. Guevara-Niebla

Introduction
Intellectuals and University Life:
Paulo Freire on Higher Education

Paulo Freire on Higher Education reflects some of the key themes of the Freirean agenda, including the relationships between education and power, curriculum in higher education, and the role of intellectuals and universities. The dialogues presented in this book took place at the National University (UNAM) in Mexico City during the first semester of 1984.

Every dialogue takes for granted a context—historical, political, and experiential—which is shared to some extent by the participants. Thus there are implicit many themes, hypotheses, assumptions, and premises, all of which structure the conversation. This dialogue between Paulo Freire and university professors in Mexico is no exception.

The purpose of this introduction is to provide the American reader with the basic historical-structural and political-symbolic context to understand even the more subtle implications of this book. We hope this introduction will help to bridge the theoretical implications of this book, deeply rooted in the Latin American tradition, with the experience of American universities, intellectuals, and students.

The academic and political life of autonomous public universities in Latin America reflects the texture and dynamics of the relationships between universities and the state. The first section, of this introduction offers a succinct yet critical appraisal of the relationships between universities and the state, highlighting three main phases: the conflict between the traditional university and the movement for educational reform of 1918; the project of the modernist university that emerges from the university reform; and the postmodernist university which is subject to the vicissitudes of the project of structural adjustment and transformation of the democratic state in the region. The second section focuses on Freire as an intellectual, in the context of debates about the university and intellectuals in Latin America. It is argued that the difficulty in classifying Freire as an intellectual results, to a large extent, from Freire's epistemological and political positions, and his own pedagogical practice celebrating the multiplicity of voices, tolerance, creativity, and open-ended dialogue.

Higher Education and the State in Latin America: Historical Background[1]

During the second half of the nineteenth century and the first three decades of the twentieth, the prevailing pact of domination in Latin America can be characterized as a form of the oligarchical state. This oligarchical state consolidated the nation and generated relative political stability. It was a political model supported by the massive exportation of agricultural products, which served to solidify the position of an oligarchy with ties to the agricultural and beef export sector of production. The dominant economic policies were anti-industriaiist and, as a general rule, the oligarchical sectors were closely linked to sectors of international capital (specially financial sectors), to which they granted concessions in diverse economic activities as one of the mechanisms by which they intended to promote economic growth and development. The oligarchy maintained tight control over the political process, on occasion by means of direct control over the state or over the parliament and important political parties. To implement this control, electoral fraud or simply open repression was employed.[2]

The oligarchical state controlled different facets of the political and cultural life of each country based upon a liberal perspective.[3] With all the variations of each national case, the Catholic church, as in Argentina attempted to establish cultural rather than political hegemony.[4] In other countries, such as Venezuela and Mexico, the power of the Catholic church was clearly attacked by the state.

The repercussions of the economic crisis and depression of 1929 brought about drastic changes in the balance of power in the world system. The decline of British hegemony and the rise of American hegemony dramatically altered the relationships between politics and economics in Latin America. The demise of the oligarchical state in the early 1930s drastically changed the political and economic landscape of the region, also affecting the universities.

With the breakdown of the oligarchical pact, a new political epoch in Latin America dawned with a new model of economic development based on import sub-stitution and new models of the state, some of them based on Keynesian policies—albeit in an embryonic stage—in different countries. Overall, what has marked the political period and historical juncture, as Collier and Collier define it,[5] are patterns of conflict and accommodation between the state and the labor movement.

The emergence of distinct forms of control and mobilization signal what Collier and Collier designate as periods of incorporation, with distinct historical legacies.

Corporativism—a set of structures that integrates society along vertical lines and as such leads to the legalization and institutionalization of the workers' movement formed and controlled by the state—appears as the distinctive characteristic of Latin American capitalism and politics in the last hundred years.

The crisis of 1929, and particularly the decay of the British Empire, drastically undermined the financial and export-oriented features of the oligarchical state. It is in this context of corporatist structures and a liberal-oligarchical state that the relationships between higher education and the state should be studied. Three university models are present in this century: the traditional university challenged by the university reform of 1918, the modernist university resulting from the reform movement, and the university emerging in the context of structural adjustment of the Latin American economies.

The University Reform Movement of 1918

Although the Catholic church had traditionally controlled the universities in Latin America, with the advent of the liberal-oligarchical state, these universities had yet to become cultural and educational centers from which a Catholic culture radiated. After the process of national reorganization and the strengthening of the liberal ideology of the new oligarchical states (with their Masonic and anticlerical perspective and clear separation between church and state), the presence of Catholic intellectuals in the public university constituted the most effective, if sparse, expression of Catholic thought in higher education. The organic intellectuals of the Argentine Church, such as José Manuel Estrada and Emilio Lamarca, can be considered paradigmatic.

The University Reform Movement of 1918 greatly influenced university and political life throughout Latin America. Starting in Córdoba on March 13, 1918, the movement quickly spread in the region; its reformist goals surpassed those of the institutional reform and had profound political implications for the transformation of conservative political regimes.[6] The reform of 1918 opposed the oligarchical university by attempting to break the ties between liberal thought and oligarchical domination and at the same time to establish the basis for a democratic legitimation of the academic task founded upon a substantial democratic consensus.

The importance of the 1918 university reform of Córdoba cannot be ignored. The reform affected the Latin American university in general and in some cases, as with Haya de la Torre y Mariátegui in Peru, its effects were felt specifically in the politics of particular countries.[7] Another example is the debate between Antonio Caso and Lombardo Toledano in Mexico.[8] This debate contrasted two types of universities, one that is politically committed (in Lombardo Toledano's proposal the university will endorse a variant of socialism), and another, (Antonio Caso's position) that relies on university autonomy and freedom of choice and speech. This debate typified many of the issues raised by the university reform, at the same time that the university began to contemplate the concurrent transformations taking place in Latin American capitalism and politics.

But what type of university does the reformist movement confront and what kind of democratic proposal does it advance? The reform confronts a university that is intimately linked to political power (from this fact stems the demand for autonomy) and that is hierarchical and conservative, with professors who receive perks and prebends with their positions or who receive said positions as a reward for their services to the conservative regime. In this patriarchical, elitist, and nepotistic university, liberal professionals use their *cátedra* (academic chairs) to give impetus to specific projects, with weak ties between serious scientific investigation and teaching.

Twenty years ago, the Brazilian anthropologist and senator Darcy Ribeiro, the first president of the innovative University of Brasilia, bitterly criticized the traditional and postreformist university as "a traditional university, federative in its organization of schools and faculties; professionalizing in its emphasis on teaching oriented toward the granting of legal degrees for liberal professionals; rigid in its curricula, established for the formation of singularly specialized professionals; stagnated because of its isolation with respect to the other institutions in society; characterized by duplicity among units in its personnel and material resources; autocratic in its government and its magisterial hierarchy of *cátedras*; bureaucratic in its dependence on the public services of the state; and elitist in its limited access and its clientelism."[9]

The University of the Democratic Modernity

The pattern of industrialization and economic development predominant in Latin America from 1940 to the 1980s was based on the following: a participation in the international market founded almost exclusively on the exportation of natural resources, an industrial structure oriented to the substitution of imports and the internal market, a model of consumption in the style of the industrialized countries, and a limited valorization of the role of the national business sector (both public and private). This pattern facilitated "a limited development of the scientific-technological endogenous base, combined with a higher education based on the 'soft' careers, of heterogenous quality and oriented toward the functions of integration of the masses."[10]

José Joaquín Brunner[11] presents an analysis in large part inspired by neo-structural functionalism[12] in the sociology of higher education, particularly the work of Burton R. Clark,[13] and Daniel Levy.[14] The transformations experienced by the institutions of higher education in Latin America, following the model of the modernist university, according to Brunner's analysis, can be summarized as follows:

1. Up until 1950 the Latin American universities were institutions of the elite. This elitism was not only determined by the social origin of students and professors—serving an elite with the cultural, educational, and the appropriate social capital—but also corresponded to the limited social function that universities served and the limited educational certification generated.[15]

2. This traditional elitist character gave the universities great cultural prestige. Furthermore, the universities had a quasimonopoly on higher education (for example, in 1959, 90.2 percent of the enrollment in higher education was in the universities). Almost all the scientific and technological investigation was carried out in the universities. The universities played a hegemonic role in the cultural arena.

3. The universities' fundamental function was professional: the formation of the elite leadership in the affairs of the state and the formation of traditional professionals, especially in medicine and law.

In the traditional institutional culture, universities revolved around the "'cátedra' in the base, with respect to the professional faculties at the institutional intermediate level, and with regard to the specific features of insertion into the arena of the state at the level of establishments."[16]

4. Up to three decades ago, therefore the universities found themselves in an incipient phase of organizational complexity: their size was not exaggerated; their teaching staffs were stable, usually consisting of liberal professionals who taught part time while working in the state or private sector; and finally, their bureaucracies were reduced to completing simple administrative tasks.

5. In the past thirty years, the universities have been transformed from institutions of the elites to universities of the masses. Around 1985, the gross rate of higher education enrollment fell from 10 percent to over 20 percent in various countries (e.g., Argentina, Ecuador, Costa Rica, Venezuela). With more than 6 million students in higher education at this time, more than half a million graduate annually—double the number who graduated thirty-five years previous. For Brunner this massification is the result of the differentiation experienced by the systems of higher education. In general, Brunner calculates that there presently are 420 universities in Latin America, absorbing close to 65 percent of all students enrolled at the tertiary or higher education level.[17] Along with the massification there has occurred an academic professionalization, with more than half a million academics working at institutions of higher learning, and more than half of these working in Brazil (123,000),

Mexico (190,000), and Argentina (65,000). In the same manner, Brunner characterizes this massification as a *mesocratization*, given the growing participation of middle and lower sectors, consistent with the arguments of the project Desarollo y Educación en América Latina y el Caribe (DEALC) directed more than a decade ago by sociologist Germán Rama. Brunner incorporates the DEALC findings that in addition to massification identify the *feminization* of the enrollment in higher education.[18] One of the causes of this feminization is the *regionalization* of higher education—the growing number of institutions of higher education established outside the metropolitan areas of the principal cities of the country and the provinces. Similarly, a *tertiarization* of enrollments, occurred, with students electing careers that pertain to the social sciences, education, commerce, and business administration. Finally, a *privatization* of the enrollment took place, reaching one-third of that in private institutions of higher education.[19]

6. For Brunner, this massification is associated with a growing differentiation, both horizontally (within each institution) and vertically (among institutions). In terms of *horizontal differentiation*, in the last three decades there has been an increase in graduate training (and its resources) to the detriment of the studies at the undergraduate level, as well as a growing investment of resources in the institutions and centers of investigation to the detriment of teaching activities in the faculties and schools. Similarly, the *vertical differentiation* has resulted in the effort to establish institutional hierarchies based on institutional tradition, quality of the

teaching staff, prestige of diplomas and titles, "internal cultural climate," and market demand.

7. Finally, these processes have brought about a greater degree of selectivity in higher education, especially in the case of Chile which Brunner analyzes: "In Chile the higher educational system tends to be highly selective from a social point of view due to the double selectiveness in terms of academics as well, which favors students with a higher level of previous educational preparation, and for having surrendered its expansion to the private sector, which makes access for students of lower income more difficult. . .the labor and artesan sectors which constitute 65 percent of the work force of the country has been represented by 21 percent in the universities with fiscal contribution and less than 2 percent in the universities without fiscal contribution."[20]

The economic crisis and fiscal crisis of the state in the eighties, the realities of the external debt of the Latin American countries[21] and the demands of the process of democratization in the context of the neoconservative policies advanced by international organizations have posed new dilemmas for Latin American universities. Whereas the modernist university faced a number of challenges including enrollment massification, questions concerning the quality and relevance of instruction, and issues of equality and/or linkages with labor markets, the answers to these problems are being advanced from neoconservative and postmodernist frameworks.[22]

The University and Structural Adjustment

During the seventies and eighties, a reorganization of the international division of labor and of capital took place. American hegemony was in decline,[23] even after the United States pushed the Soviet Union to bankruptcy with the arms race. Japan and Germany have emerged as powerful economic competitors of the postwar era. The international exchange has taken on unprecedented dimensions, particularly with the announcement of the project of unification of Europe in 1992 and the creation of a common market between Canada, Mexico and the United States. International economies have become integrated to a surprising extent: it is difficult for the United States, for example, to determine the American component of an automobile produced in a plant in Kentucky. The highly successful experiences of NICs (newly industrialized countries)—specifically Korea, Taiwan, Hong Kong, and Singapore—based on low-cost production are a model for "latecomers" to the international system. Global strategies of production in multinational companies have created a more economically and politically interdependent world, with strong pressures to cut back on the value of the labor force and with the replacement of the Keynesian economic formulas. Alliances between labor and capital have grown increasingly difficult in the context of industrial reorganization. New economic orthodoxies—predominantly "trickle down" economies—and market ideologies have permeated the capitalist world and are begining to be experienced in the new open markets because of the downfall of *real* socialism in the former Soviet Union and in Eastern Europe.

In Latin America the external debt and the limitations of domestic capital accumulation forced the new and old democracies, this time with predominantly neoliberal governments, to adopt the economic policy dictates of the International Monetary Fund with all its conditionalities. Other important phenomena are the decline of the state sector and its participation in the fixed gross investment rate in Latin America; the reorientation of economic policies from production for an internal market toward production for an international market; the growth of a more sophisticated middle class, linked to the international system and highly differentiated and stratified; the diminishing (demographically as well as in terms of political power) of the peasantry and working classes and the growth of marginal urban sectors and of informal labor markets. These conditions characterize what Collier and Collier call the advent of a new political juncture in the region.[24]

The crisis of 1979—produced by the rise in the price of petroleum and the recession of 1981–82 in the United States, which profoundly affected countries such as Costa Rica and Mexico whose economies are closely linked to the United States—generated an economic whirlwind in Latin America, which manifested itself in problems with the external debt and the fiscal affairs of the state. To restore economic development, bridge loans from the International Monetary Fund and structural adjustment loans (SAL) from the World Bank were extensively implemented in Latin America, with Brazil, being the last country to sign an agreement with the IMF in July of 1992.

Structural adjustment imposes a number of conditions, including the reduction of government expenditure, devaluations to promote exports, reduction in import tariffs, and the increase in public and private savings. The policies of structural adjustment also include the reduction of the fiscal deficit at the same time as public expenditure is reduced and strict monetary policies are applied to lower inflation. Some of the consequences of this model are the absolute reduction of the state sector, the liberalization of salaries and prices, and the reorientation of industrial and agricultural production toward exportation.[25] The combined pressure of the conditionalities of the IMF and World Bank loans and the financing difficulties created by the external debt crisis have generated new educational policies of the region.[26]

There are new efforts to pass the costs of these services on to the clientele by increasing the participation of the private sector in education (i.e., privatization), by reorienting educational investments toward areas of study that the World Bank has considered to render the greatest rates of return (i.e., primary education and basic education) by reducing the cost of education, (which affects salary levels and for that matter teacher training—teachers are considered overeducated and their university training leads them to have higher salary expectations than what the countries can finance[27]) and by promoting a deconcentration and or decentralization of educational services as a means of redefining the power and educational relations among national (federal), provincial, and municipal governments.[28]

At the time that this conversation between Freire and university professors took place at the UNAM in Mexico City in 1984, the process of structural adjustment and drastic changes of the Latin American states were just beginning. Thus, to understand the unity in the diversity of topics, themes, and discussions presented in this book, we need to understand the historical, structural, and political background presented above. It is evident that political changes affecting the universities not only transform academic work, but also drastically modify the relationships between intellectuals and higher education institutions. The next section discusses the role of intellectuals and Paulo Freire's views.

Paulo Freire, Universities, and Intellectuals in Latin America

Paulo Freire graduated from the University of Recife in Pernambuco with a degree in law. After a short period of working as a lawyer—he tried only one case—he accepted in 1946 a position with the Social Service of Industry (Serviço Social da Induústria), an institution created in his native Recife by the private sector with clear reformist goals.[29] Freire worked for eight years at SESI, becoming director of the educational sector. In 1959 he applied for an academic position as chair of history and philosophy of education at the University of Recife. Following the Brazilian system for appointments at the professorial level, which is organized along similar lines to the German system, Freire wrote his dissertation entitled "Educação e atualidade brasileira," ("Education and Brazilian Reality"], obtaining the equivalent of a doctorate but losing the academic position. He remained with an appointment as technician (adjunct faculty) at the university level, becoming the first director of the Service of Extension (Serviço de Extensão Cultural) of the University of Recife, where he had his first experiences with literacy training and adult education.

Freire's work in Recife attracted national attention when he was appointed in 1963 as director of the National Program for Literacy Training launched by the populist government of João Goulard. The coup d'etat of 1964 ended the literacy training experiment. Freire was incarcerated for seventy days and ultimately exiled. He returned to Brazil in 1980. Freire had taught in Brazilian universities before 1964. In exile, however, although he lectured all over the world, he collaborated only marginally with universities, teaching occasionally, as at

Harvard for a semester in 1969 or at the University of Geneva sporadically from 1970 to 1979. After his return to Brazil in 1980, Freire secured an academic position at the University of Campinas, and at the Catholic University, both in São Paulo. Despite his experience and reputation, it is only in the last twelve years that Paulo Freire has become an academic, fully engaged in graduate teaching, research, and extension in Brazilian universities, and spending short periods as a distinguished professor at American, Canadian, and European universities. But what kind of academic is Paulo Freire?

Joseph Maier and Richard W. Weatherhead in their introduction to *The Latin American University*, express very clearly a conventional view held in the United States regarding Latin American academics:

> Professors are not wholly academic creatures; they retain only part-time posts in the university while performing other professional work on the outside. Teaching is a demanding exercise and monetarily an unrewarding one. The professor does receive compensations, however: he is considered a *maestro* or becomes one, revered and honored by students. Such reverence, however, often is accorded him not because of the incisive brilliance of his lectures but rather because of his ideological zeal and oratory. The professor as well as the intellectual must have the gift of the word; he must be a rhetorician, harking back to his scholastic forebears of the sixteenth and seventeenth centuries.[30]

In this view, university professors are rhetoricians, more sophists than philosophers, and certainly not scholars pursuing objective, rigorously scientific and politically neutral research and teaching agendas in the calm environment of their laboratories or offices: university professors in Latin America are merely intellectuals as well as ideologues and polemicists. They are marked by the corporatist cultural structures of the Iberian societies, remaining captives of their authoritarian, hierarchical, Machiavellian, and Thomist past:

> The Latin American intellectual is an ideologue and polemicist, and influences the university because of the reach of his ideas and the glitter of his prose and poetry. The *pensador* of the nineteenth century and the intellectual of the twentieth century write of the glories and unity of the Latin races. They are beacons for a whole generation, whether that of 1898, 1918, or any other epochal year. . . . The intellectual today is a more professional critic of society than was the *pensador*. He is also more cosmopolitan, and his criticism more widely read. Intellectuals do not always associate themselves with partisan callings as did the *pensadors*. All wrote extensively, and virtually no subject was foreign to their pen. They addressed themselves to their generation and to the young of the next, exhorting them to fulfill their ideals and to found the perfect society. The fact that the Latin American *pensador*—and on occasion the intellectual—so often take the road of exile attests to the political force of their writings. Governments fear the effects of their hortatory presence on the internal political process and the influence of their voice upon students and professor partisanships."[31]

From this perspective, the academic profession in Latin America is described as a melange of politicism, rhetoric, activism, and encyclopedism practiced by part-time professors who are at the same time full-time liberal professionals or state bureaucrats. They are, in short, ideological zealots who construct their careers and the social imaginary by resorting to their powerful oratory, prose, and poetry. They are either *pensadores, intellectuals,* or *doctrinaires,* but certainly not *scholars,* because they lack the scholar's professional ethics, scientific practices, and commitment to research and teaching as a full-time profession.

This is not the place to assess whether the distinction between pensadores, intellectuals, and scholars is a useful one. It is commonplace to define as a scholar someone who has esoteric expertise in a scientific, humanistic, technical, or cultural domain, and who has proven this expertise by conducting research that is sanctioned as acceptable by his or her peers according to the rules of the academic community and norms of science. One may take exception with such a definition of scholarship if it masks the political implications of scientific work, neglects the intersubjective evaluation of academic work as a proxy for an elusive scientific objectivity, or simply if scholarly work is considered exclusively as a technocratic practice, rigorously regulated and legislated through standardized rules of professions or disciplines. Likewise, one may take exception with any sharp distinction between scholars and intellectuals as representing mutually exclusive or incommensurable practices (and roles) in society.

From a Marxist perspective, James Petras has sharply criticized what he considers the metamorphosis of Latin American intellectuals.[32] Petras sees two diametrically opposed intellectuals in Latin America: the *organic intellectual* in the Gramscian sense of the sixties, and the *institutional intellectual* of the eighties.[33] In the sixties, writers, journalists, and political economists "linked directly to political and social struggles against imperialism and capitalism. They were integral parts of trade unions, students movements, or revolutionary parties."[34] Most of these intellectuals were either killed, jailed, exiled, or expelled from universities by dictatorships, and those who remained alive lost their souce of income. Petras sees that this class of intellectuals "was politically and economically vulnerable and increasingly disposed to accept external funding as a mode of survival."[35] Thus, for Petras, a perverse combination of economic need and dependency, the pressure of international public opinion, and the changes in funding criteria and liberalized ideological criteria of private faundations, government aid agencies, and social democratic parties in metropolitan countries gave birth to institutional intellectuals in Latin America—a new, internationally oriented intellectuals who may be critics of the neoliberal economic model but who are "deeply embedded in dependent relations with overseas networks" and who by serving as regime advisors in the new democracies "shifted their research agenda away from critical studies of inequalities, dependence, and power, toward technocratic and developmental directions."[36] For Petras, they, as regime apologists, have abdicated their responsibilities as critical intellectuals.[37]

A distinction between organic and institutional intellectuals may not be entirely useful. Petras employs a fairly deterministic and economicist perspective. He is unable to explain why in more stable countries, such as Mexico or Venezuela, many of the intellectuals he would have surely considered as organic in the sixties, could be considered according to his typology as institutional intellectuals in the eighties. Petras's analysis simply does not account for the fundamental cultural tranformation of the Latin American societies, a transformation associated with the concept of postmodernism. To argue that these changes are prompted merely by an ideological capitulation to the economic security of academic life is simply an ad hominem argument based on a simplistic and reductionist perception of the complexities of academic life.[38]

Freire comes from a liberal-democratic Catholic tradition, clearly associated with the modernist, anti-traditional university. His writings from the sixties and seventies criticize the narrow views of specialization (*specialisms* in Freire's terminology) and support the notion of engaged intellectuals in critical dialogue with the people, learning about and from people's knowledge. He has repeatedly criticized *scienticism*—those scientific practices that fail to recognize the conflicts in society, particularly class conflicts. He has emphasized the linkages between politics, education, and, by implication, academic work. He has emphasized that for him, teaching is the act of knowing, and learning involves a subjective stance: "It is impossible that a person, not being the subject of his own curiosity, can truly grasp the object of his knowledge."[39]

Freire's academic, gnosiological, and political approach has proven ethically consistent. He has always emphasized that the first commitment of an intellectual is a complete docility toward the reality that is to be studied, described, and explained in a particular theoretical and historical context. This docility is not a call for empiricism but, on the contrary, it is an invitation to listen to the multiple voices that articulate and constitute the experience, knowledge, and consciousness of the oppressed, of those who hardly have had any systematic education to facilitate learning about their own experience. For Freire, this experience is the beginning of the construction of knowledge, which should be supplemented with the theoretical rigor of the social sciences in critic dialogue with the living experience of the people. That is the reason that in his early and insightful writings of the sixties, Freire called for an epistemological approach that facilitates the archeology of consciousness—that is an approach through which learning to name the world helps people to change the world. That is the reason that for Freire, literacy consists of a set of practices that either empowers or disempowers people. Indeed, Freire argues in this book that "if we are not able to talk about their [students'] common experience, turning it into philosophy, then we do not know what to do with our science."[40]

Freire has argued that every book he has written is a report of a particular phase of his pedagogical and political experience. Even writing his famous *Pedagogy of the Oppressed* in Chile "appeared as a practical, theoretical necessity in my professional career."[41] Writing about his own political and pedagogical praxis, usually at the margins of academic activities in the modernist universities of the sixties, Freire has always claimed to be a radical but never a sectarian—a very important distinction in the context of the complexities of the political struggle of Latin America in the sixties and seventies.

Despite his self-definition as a radical, in a famous interview with members of a socialist journal in Chile in 1972,[42] Freire was accused of not using class analysis or not giving enough weight to class struggle in his writings. Similarly, his interviewers implied that his emphasis on freedom and democracy will make him a liberal intellectual, thus putting him at odds with the revolutionary project.

In a recent visit to post-Pinochet Chile, twenty years after that interview, Freire's insistency on the importance of class for political and educational practices caused reactions in many intellectual circles, and he was accused of being a romantic, bringing back "themes" of the sixties. Freire commented laconically that although he still resorts to class analysis and although the concepts of democracy and freedom are key elements of his research and pedagogical agenda, many of his critics of the sixties have drastically switched positions.[43]

Freire cannot be easily classified as an organic intellectual of the sixties in Petras's taxonomy nor can he be accused of being an institutional intellectual. Freire's experience as secretary of education of the municipality of São Paulo between 1989 and 1991 took place under the rubric of a socialist and democratically elected Workers Party (Partido dos Trabalhadores), a rara avis political experience in the context of neoliberal governments in Latin America.

Freire is a different kind of intellectual. His emphasis on an epistemology or theory of knowledge as a precondition to learning, his perception that every pedagogical act is a political act, and his criticism of the notion of intellectual as scholar narrowly defined as a specialist situates Freire in the tradition of the nineteenth-century Latin American pensadores while embracing many of the themes of the critical intellectual that emerge with the movement for reform of 1918, becoming more radicalized with the revolutionary experiences of the sixties and early seventies. His research and practical agenda transcends the modernist university, however, and the reverberations of his work reach postmodern criticism.

Against the dry pragmatism and *realpolitik* of the nineties, Freire still proposes ethical and political principles that are tied to the modernity project (fairness, justice, empowerment, love) while also criticizing the incompleteness of the modernist process and the appropriateness of many postmodernist criticisms. He argues that "we cannot enter into the struggle for the transformation of society ignoring the fact that the dominant class has an extraordinary power to 'folklorize' the most advanced ideas. . . . For me the point is not to stop using words such as *curiosity* or *creativity*, only because the dominating class has started to use them; I also think that it is absurd to stop using the word *love*. There is no revolution without love; the revolution is loving. The fact that the bourgeoisie has distorted an important word has nothing to do with me."[44]

His emphasis on a loving revolution shows that Freire is at the same time a traditional, a modernist, and a postmodernist intellectual, and he cannot be easily classified as a romantic or a pragmatic intellectual or put into the straitjacket taxonomy of organic versus institutional intellectuals.

What is fascinating about the discussion in this book is that Freire's arguments result from his perspective as an academic in Brazilian universities but also as an intellectual linked politically to a socialist party. Compared to his experiences as secretary of education four years later, the consistency of his message, his approach to learning and knowing, and his principles of *realpolitik* linked to a possible utopia for social change show no mutation.

The democratization of higher education and Mexican society in general was a substantial part of the workshop's agenda—a theme clearly present in the crisis of 1968 and the contribution of the student movements. This is a fundamental issue, particularly because some of the intellectuals whom Freire encountered in this debate were political activists, trade union activists, and university students in the sixties and seventies, and because the debates about the university and academic policy were beginning to show the impact of postmodernist criticism but also of the implementation of the neoliberal and neoconservative political agenda in the region.

Critical views of democracy and the academic profession predominate. There are discussions about the degree of authoritarianism of university trade unions, the complacency of a conformist culture among university professors, and the lack of a truly democratic discussion about the role of the university in the process of change in Mexico or Latin America. There is also the claim that university professors are out of touch with reality, even if some of them claim to follow a Freirean epistemology of starting from the real and concrete:

> Most professors do not address objective reality. Rather, they address analysis of objective reality found in books and articles. They turn this into the object of knowledge, within struggle for power, focusing upon accumulated knowledge. This impedes approximation to reality. The learning exercise is turned into a struggle around representations that we have of reality, and ideological struggle, addressing power that we do know how to manipulate. Consequently, the dialogue that should emerge from such analysis is no longer a mediated dialogue leading to reality. It is an alienating metaphysical "dialogue" about an abstract "reality" that has no real meaning.[45]

Despite the criticism of metaphysics, the notion of an "objective reality" appears as a demiurge that can be apprehended through the mediation of true dialogue, a dialogue not about "representations," but about true reality. Another premise is that the knowledge of this "objective reality" in its entire concreteness can be reached without resorting to abstraction. As a response, Freire emphasizes the importance of dialogue, but claims that there is no historicity in the academy that can be construed outside the global political context. Respect for political pluralism in the university is another tool for constructing the understanding of objective reality by respecting multiple voices. This is not intended to belittle the risks involved in creativity, however, nor does it prevent intellectuals and scholars from sustaining political views:

> This is a call for nothing less than an experience of risk within an academy that does not sacrifice itself because it does not take the risk of creating. There is no creativity without the risk of creating. . . . The matter of freedom is basic for the search, for risk. However, we cannot fall into a naive idealism when thinking that it is possible to create a "province of freedom" outside a specific society where the material conditions of that society work against the affirmation of freedom.[46]

From a naive perspective, the tolerance, freedom, and respect predicated in Freire's view of intellectuals and the academic environment do not seem to agree with intellectuals becoming politically engaged, taking risks, or developing open-ended dialogues as a tool for intellectual inquiry. Nor does it agree with the challenge to university professors who may be prisoners of the Cartesian discourse, detached from the idea of praxis. Freire's legacy and his dialectical thinking and emphasis on dialogue, however, show a more complex understanding of the relationships between university life, academic policies, and politics. While emphasizing the notions of curiosity, creativity, and risk taking as essential attributes for intellectual inquiry, Freire also argues that when he started not to be sure of his own certainty, he realized that he has become more sure, because the only way one may have to be sure is by not being sure. This is perhaps the reason why he cannot be easily classified as a traditional, modernist, or postmodern intellectual.

Freire's dialectical views of intellectuals and the role of university are inspired by what he considered the great lesson of his exile: "One thing I also learned in exile, maybe the best thing I ever learned, is that I could not continue being sure of my certainty."[47] This is obviously a lesson for every intellectual and for the pursuit of academic work.

Carlos Alberto Torres

1

Education and Power

Questions about Power and Social Change

G. Guevara-Niebla: My reflections and my questions are directed toward what would be the key points in a theory of power.

In reading the main works of Freire, we notice that he was able to achieve a break with a very long-standing theoretical tradition that preached pessimism in education. In other words, Freirian thinking surpassed the theories and explanations that related any exercise in education in an automatic and fatal manner to domination. Education was destined only to serve domination and the reproduction of the forms of domination. Instead, in Freire—and it seems to me that this has been his fundamental contribution to universal Latin American education—we discover a horizon and an optimistic perspective from which education can be recovered as an instrument of liberation, as a means of questioning the established forms of power. When examining this revolutionary idea, it is natural that some basic questions should immediately arise: how is social change, that is, revolution, perceived within this new perspective? This is the axial problem in Paulo Freire's proposal. In reading his work and becoming acquainted with some experiences related to his propositions, such as the literacy campaigns during the Goulart period and the popular culture movement in Brazil, we realize that the practice of education revolves around the teacher-student relationship, as an interchange, a bringing together of particular subjects, and on a wider scope, an encounter of the educator or educators with a community.

What is meant here by social change? Two different kinds of questions arise. Is it possible to achieve or hope for a global change in society born of a particular pedagogic exercise, be it at the individual level or on a community level? In addition, is it possible to imagine social change arising from this single sphere, the educational sphere? In any case, how can the practice of social change in education be linked with the activity of change that operates or can operate in other spheres of society? At any rate, who is the subject of social change? In other words, in the Marxist critical tradition, the subject, as we all know, is identified with the social classes; in the case of modern revolution, with the proletariat. We ask ourselves which is the subject of social change within Freire's thinking, and from the perspective of carrying out social change, we arrive naturally and logically at the problem of the political party. Is it possible to imagine revolutionary action within society on the fringe of what traditionally have been the structures of political power, such as the parties? Is it possible to conceive of the development of a revolutionary change without the political parties? And finally, the last question that comes to my mind at this time is in relation to the case of the state and the concept of political power within society.

At first instance, we always try to relate Freire to Gramsci. Gramsci postulated that every pedagogic relationship holds a hegemonic relationship; a pedagogical relationship involves a relationship of power, of domination, but a domination conceived of not exclusively as coercion, not only as an external exercise of power, but also and basically as a consensus, as a conquest of the active will of the subordinated classes or of the masses.

From the perspective of Gramsci or if we try to join this Gramscian proposal with Freire's postulates, we will necessarily ask ourselves what is the project of intellectual and moral reform, what is the conception of the world proposed by Freire in exercising or putting into practice a revolutionary pedagogy, in establishing a liberating pedagogic relationship. So, these are the general problems that are implicated.

Pedagogism in Freire?

P. Freire: I will attempt to give a speech, which probably is not very well organized. I shall try to ponder some of the main points that have been exposed. I do not think that I answered your questions correctly with my reflections, but I shall try to express what I am thinking and I will probably repeat some things that have already been wxpressed in my papers or texts published from 1978 to 1981. I believe that an interview that I gave in 1973 had something to do with the questions that you raised; nevertheless, I will probably say something that I did not write, that I am writing now, but as I am alive it is legitimate for me to say something today for the first time; it would be wonderful and it would be my right because I am alive. You are talking about something with which I agree completely: that I proposed a certain optimism in relation to the task of education. But the fundamental problem is to know what kind of optimism this would be, because in proposing an optimistic, hopeful point of view toward education I could also lapse into a certain "pedagogism"—that is, a naive optimism as concerns the practice of education.

Within the "pedagogistic" perspective, you would change or reduce all transformation to pedagogy, and this has something to do with one of your questions: I think that I did not lapse into pedagogism, which to me would be regrettable, yet some of my critics say that I made that mistake, that I have reduced revolutionary transformation to education. In other words, they mean to say that I made a mistake when I considered education to be the lever for revolutionary transformation. Even Francisco Weffort says this, in his preface to my first book, *Educación como practica de la libertad* [Paulo Freire. La educación como práctica de la libertad. Mexico, Slgloxxi Editores, 1969.] which is really a very naive book, but in its naïveté pointed out some criticisms. I think that certain critics are mistaken when they are not capable of perceiving the dialectics between naïveté and "criticity," when they cannot perceive certain naïvetés.

This was one of the texts that I wrote in 1977, and I either rewrote or added things that were not originally included, for example, among others, an old university thesis that I had written in 1958 or 1959, because I was never inclined to believe that education could be the lever for revolution, precisely because I was absolutely convinced of something that in the 1970s seemed very well defined, very much emphasized, which was the reproducing role of school, of systematic education, the reproducing role of the dominant ideology, the ideology in power.

Education and Social Reproduction

But my optimistic position is nowadays more clearly defined in the following: I am also absolutely convinced that the main task of systematic education is the reproduction of the ideology of the dominant class, that of reproducing the conditions for the preservation of their power, but precisely because the relationship between systematic education, as a subsystem, and the social system, is one of opposition and mutual contradiction. Therefore, when talking about reproduction as the task of the dominant class, there is the possibility of counteracting the task of reproducing the dominant ideology. So it seems to me that we see what happens, the level or grade of education is unimportant; whether it be preschool or the university or postgraduate school, we clearly perceive a permanent movement, very dynamic and contradictory, between the task of reproduction and that of counteracting the reproduction. These two tasks are dialectic: one is the task of the system, the other is ours; therefore, it is determined by the system but not requested by it. The system believes that it obtains from education one of the fundamental instruments for the reproduction of its power, and so dialectically, necessarily, must create its antagonist; its antagonistic opposite, as a revolutionary task, belongs to us.

Transformation and Institutional Space

Now, it is important to know how and when we occupy the institutional spaces in order to fulfill the task of counterattacking the reproducing role of systematic education. Obviously, it is easy to perceive that it is quite simple to fulfill the task established by the system. To reproduce dominant ideology is the same thing as swimming with the tide; to assume the role of counterattacking the reproduction of dominant ideology is to swim against the tide. Therefore, to use the space in favor of reproduction is one thing, and to use the space against reproduction is quite another. It seems to me that another very important point is being brought up here, which is the power relationship, since it is not possible to think of education without thinking about power. I think this point is central to any consideration concerning the task of reproduction and the task of counterattacking the reproductive task itself, of those whose political dream is the transformation of society and not the reproduction and preservation of bourgeois society.

The task of counteracting is proposed to those who humbly accept it, knowing that this is not the lever, and from here I come to a proposal made by Gilberto Guevara: the issue of the critical and dialectic comprehension of the relationship between practice and strategy.

From my point of views an educator whose political option is the transformation of bourgeois society in favor of the interests of the popular working social classes, but who does not think of devoting a his or her time, through his or her own experience, to ponder on the manner in which practices and strategies are related, cannot function correctly.

If you take strategy, for example, aware of the place where you are putting your dream, the possible dream that is not yet materialized, I think that what we have here is still a dream that is yet to come true—that of the transformation of the present time. If your dream is in your strategy, the purpose of your struggle, you have to find the ways that will make the materialization of your dream possible, and those ways are precisely the tactics, the means, which you even have to create.

Furthermore, the issue which has been brought up is that of the eminently historical nature of these means. On the one hand, these means, these practices, have to be related or tuned into the strategy, to the dream; in other words, I cannot have a dream of liberation and use a means of domestication, not in my opinion. And it seems to me that this is one of the most serious problems that we have as intellectuals, not being consistent or coherent, frequently not living in coherence between discourse and practice; we make a speech in behalf of our dream, of an eminently revolutionary strategy, but our practice is reactionary. For example, with the students and the people, we declare ourselves the proprietors of science and of the revolution, and we denounce the lack of conscience of the working class, and yet we say that we have the conscience of a class to which we do not belong; this is slightly crazy and cannot be.

The relation between practice and strategy cannot always be the same. For example, it is one thing to work, to create your own working tactics at a lower level, such as the one that we are talking about, and another thing to do it at a higher level, in a political party, for example, but this is quite different for Mexico from what it would be for Brazil. The fact that a certain procedure has worked well in a given society does not give me the authority to say that if transplanted to another society, sometimes to another time, it will be the same thing. It is necessary to make a historical reading of the texts; we must read Lenin, but we must situate him in time and in space, the space and the time in which he wrote. This does not mean that you have to change everything completely, but you have to lend your time and your space.

The Revolution is Pedagogic

This issue is absolutely fundamental if one does not lapse into pedagogism, if one does not accept that education is not the lever for transformation. Nonetheless, there is a space, however small, in the practice of education, in the educative system as a subsystem; there is a minimum space that we must use to our advantage.

I return to the same issue as you did, Gilberto, when you were asking if it is possible to consider a global, radical transformation of society through education. I have already seen that it is not possible, but we must think a bit more; education is not the lever of transformation, of revolution, and yet revolution is pedagogic, and I am not playing with words. There is a pedagogic testimony in the practice of social transformation; it is the process of mobilization which is automatically also a process of organization. There is no mobilization without organization, so to differentiate one from the other seems to me naive; it is not dialectic, since one does not first mobilize and subsequently organize. The essence of mobilization itself contains organization; the process of organizational mobilization is profoundly pedagogic.

For example, in Brazil, during the so-called direct elections, we held the first meeting for elections in January 1984, and the political leaderships of the parties were not very convinced that the popular masses would respond in a positive manner to the invitation to go out into the streets and the public spaces to discuss the need to have direct elections. Nevertheless, 300,000 people were present at the first central meeting, and the leaderships, even those of the Workers Party, to which I belong, did not expect this; it was an extraordinary and complete challenge.

In April of that year during the last popular meeting before the elections, 1,700,000 people gathered in the streets of São Paulo, singing the national anthem, joining hands. Newspaper releases stated that they did not damage even one flower; 1,700,000 people went out into the streets demanding direct vote, and they spoiled nothing. The city remained just as before or even better, because it was impregnated with the people.

This mobilization process was highly pedagogic, and yet there was no previous curriculum, no established schedule; it just happened, without being "spontaneistic" either, because there was a political leadership that invited the masses to demand. This fact in itself is political, and because it is political, it is pedagogic. There is a "politicity" in education, in the same way that there is an "educatability" in that which is political; in other words, there is a political nature in education, just as there is a pedagogic nature in political action, and this, to me, is quite impressive. During one period I no longer spoke about it; for example, in *Educación como pràctica de la libertad*, there is no mention of the political aspect. Some time ago, I started talking about the political dimension of education and I state that there is no political dimension, that there is no politicity in education; in other words, education itself is of a political nature, just as politics in itself is of a pedagogical nature. The point is to know in which direction the political aspect of the education that you practice is headed, the direction of the education contained in the politics that you establish in the streets, in other words, that which is proposed by your party, whose side your politics are on, at whose service or against whom your work as an educator, and therefore as a politician, is directed.

I have thought a great deal about this during the last three or four years and I was asking myself: could it be that there is no certain specificity of that which is pedagogic, of that which is political? Recently a Brazilian professor, a young Gramscian philosopher, said: "Education seeks to convince and politics seeks to win, therefore in any educative action there is conviction and in any political action there is victory, and therein lies the specificity of one and the other." I do not agree. For example, for a left-wing party, the moment of victory must pass through the moment of convincing the popular masses; obviously a left-wing party does not intend to convince the dominating class. For this reason, the left-wing party does not need to educate the dominating class unless it is indirectly, but a left-wing party must have a pedagogic relationship, and therefore one of conviction, with the popular masses. A right-wing party cannot convince us, and in my opinion, does not intend to convince the popular masses, through the knowledge of reality, which cannot be seen naked by the masses unless the right wing, and therefore the dominating class, takes a very great risk.

But this dimension of manipulation is also pedagogic, because if you accept that education is education only when it is liberating, then you lapse into a certain purism, and I confess that it is hard for me to admit that a manipulating pedagogy should be called education, that a manipulative practice should be called education, but I do consider it as such.

Educative Manipulation

There is no liberating education without some measure of manipulation; there is no such thing as angelical purity. The important thing is to know which is the predominant space between liberation and manipulation; that is the issue. Continuing our reflection on specificity and when we think of ourselves, when you are in a seminar, discussing with the students, you are obviously in the perspective of convincing, but this act of convincing that you carry out as a pedagogic task in the university transcends the walls of the university, as a function of your political option within a political society. In reality, when you work toward convincing the students, your effort is in relation to a political victory that takes place outside of the university. Your act of convincing seeks to obtain support for your greater dream, not simply to be a good professor. If you accept that your teachings do not go beyond the walls, in my opinion you are making a mistake, that of elitism. You will be a Marxist who only knows Marx through books and who restricts Marxism to the classroom, outside of which he claims to be only an academic. This is denying Marx and denying education itself.

Another issue that you have pointed out in relation to this is the role of the parties, which also includes the role of the vanguards, for example, as regards the comprehension of what the vanguard is. Because there are different ways of understanding the vanguards, and also the leaderships and the relationships between the political relationships, which are also pedagogic, as well as their relationship with the working class, with the popular masses. You can have an authoritarian approach to understanding the role of leaderships, or you can have a democratic approach. I think that as men and women of the left, we must not fear the word *democracy*, as if it were inevitably linked to the bourgeoisie or to social democracy.

Democracy and Knowledge

It is obvious that without organization, without theory, without discipline, without effort, without reflection about permanent practice, there can be no revolution. I have always said that revolution also is closely related to epistemology. Revolution is not guessing, although there is a guessing dimension within revolution. Revolution is something very serious, precisely because it involves the issue of power, and the party is a fundamental vehicle for mobilization, for putting into practice the revolutionary dream. Just thinking out loud, without trying to make any categorical statements: one thing that began to trouble me during the 1970s when I was in Europe, in relation to the parties, was the sometimes chaotic and sometimes overwhelming surfacing of popular social movements of rebellion.

I recall that in conversations with some fellow friends of the left in Europe during the 1970s, talking for example about the women's rights movements, the gay and the ecologists' movements, I said that in my opinion, there is something new, historic, which is beginning to appear, and that this will be related to a new way of understanding the role of the political parties. Some of my comrades said that it was foolish to think that, because these movements do not speak of class struggle. I myself felt that Marx must be understood in a Marxist manner, that is, we must not immobilize Marx; that would be profoundly antidialectic and antihistorical. Furthermore, in the world today one should not try to reduce everything that happens, even drinking a cup of coffee, to class struggle. One should understand the different moments in which class struggle manifests itself in the city, but in a dual manner, and in my opinion those movements of this decade are going to bring something into our politics, which is going to demand that we reformulate, or at least find a different, more historical way of thinking of the role of the parties. At that time I used to say that it was necessary to look beyond, and discover in the intimacy and the dynamics of those movements, the appearance of a new popular education. To a great extent the new popular education, the politics of this education, are being born in those movements, and not in our seminars or in our books. I said at that time that the left-wing parties should come closer and closer to those movements, but without trying to take them over.

The Reinvention of Power and the Popular Movements

Today, if you observe what is taking place, for example, in France, the ecologists contributed 1,500,000 votes toward Mitterand's election. I do not wish to discuss if they now regret it or not, that is another issue; what the ecologists did in Germany.

In my opinion, the critical comprehension of these popular movements faces us today as a fundamental task for a political scientist and for an educator in this position. It is evident that those popular movements are not yet the means to obtain political power; they need the parties, which in turn must realize that the movements will continue to be legitimate means to reach power.

If you analyze the political situation in Brazil today, you will find two new situations, very recent in the political history of Brazil. One of these new situations is the ecclesiastic base communities. If one does not fully comprehend Marx's fundamental criticism of religion, I think that at this point in history it is not possible to understand what is happening in our societies. I do not mean by this that we should change the Materialists, the Marxists, and that they should all become converted now to Christianity, nothing of the sort. But what is fundamental is to comprehend, historically, the historicity of religion, and not in a metaphysical sense. We must understand in a Marxist sense, dialectically and not metaphysically, the role of the ecclesiastic base communities, which have presented an extraordinary challenge to the Brazilian military government. The second situation is that of the union struggles, born precisely of the workers.

Today, if the Workers' Party, approaches the popular movements from which it was born, without trying to take them over, the party will grow; if it turns away from the popular movements, in my opinion, the party will wear down. Besides, those movements need to make their struggle politically viable.

I will leave with you one of my concerns for which I have no answer, and I bring it forth here as a challenge that I feel and that you probably feel as well; perhaps later on one of you will delve into it more deeply. This challenge emerges at the level of politics, of praxis at the end of this century, before those of us who pursue a revolutionary transformation of bourgeois society in order to install a socialist society. In my opinion, one of the basic themes of the end of the century is not the issue of taking power in itself, as much as the reinvention of power, and this includes the dialectic comprehension of the role of the political parties.

What I mean to say by this is that for me the most important thing is not to seize bourgeois power, in spite of all that means in terms of power. Regardless of the question of whether the bourgeoisie consciously or unconsciously elaborated its own ideology during centuries of experience, bourgeois power was transferred from one society to another according to a practice well rooted in the institutional structures of bourgeois society. But suddenly a revolution arose, to seize this power, and in doing this, without inventing it, people think magically that the simple fact of an infrastructural transformation will decree a noble conception of power. To me, this is mechanical and not dialectic, and here we come to another issue, another problem that has to do with the end of the century, in the sense that there is a return not to pre-Hegelian idealistic subjectivism nor to a different objectivist subjectivism, but instead to a comprehension of the role of subjectivity in history, in its dialectic relationship with objectivity.

With this I propose not only the issue of seizing power, but that of the reinvention of power as one of the fundamental themes for a critical left, which cannot be afraid of thinking about what it is going to do with the power obtained, not even at the most difficult moment of revolutionary transition, when the revolution comes to power and is faced with an entire apparatus that was created before the revolution, obviously by the bourgeoisie.

Revolutionary Education

At this stage of the transition, if one considers only the content of education, in the societies that I visited I encountered an invitation to put revolutionary processes into practice. In other words, the revolution that reaches power needs to create a new society, which cannot appear by decree but rather appears before History; it needs to create, to assist in the birth of the new society, and this process of birth of the new society has in revolutionary education, once the revolution is in power, an indispensable, fantastic aid. One thing is our work today, against the bourgeois system, and yet another will be our work in a revolutionary corps, to create through education. See how different things are, because if in the bourgeois system education has as its main task the reproduction of bourgeois ideology, with the revolution in power our task is precisely that of creating a new ideology, a new foundation. To the extent that we are not idealists in the philosophical sense, we believe that the latter kind of education cannot be decreed if the new society that is in accordance with it does not yet exist.

In the transition stage there is no new society; there is only a society of transition. The new, revolutionary education does not yet exist, and cannot exist. At this stage, bourgeois education is no longer acceptable, because it has nothing to do with the formation of the new revolutionary society, but you still do not have the new education because you are as yet lacking time in space for its creation. This for me has to do with the question of power, because if we make any mistakes we run the risk of immobilizing the revolution, in a certain sense.

Pedagogy of Transition

G. Guevara-Niebla: I think that we can reach a new development in our meeting. It is evident that the problematic involved in the relationship between education and power is a very broad problem that we could not cover or discuss completely in a minimum working session such as this one. But perhaps we could use it to maximum advantage by directing our meeting toward some problems that we consider of relevance to all of us. A first aspect that derives from the position that we just heard is that it implies a descent from the more general level to particular aspects. For example, in relation to the last part of what Paulo was saying to us, about the nature of political power in society and the need of conceiving a "transition pedagogy," so to speak, one asks oneself if this transition is already formulated in the proposals that have been made within the pedagogy of liberation, or if it is just beginning to be built on the basis of these proposals, or if this transition pedagogy should be elaborated a posteriori, in the future, to be generated in the moment that follows the takeover of political power.

In essence, the implicit problem is a strategy of revolutionary change: that of the role that would be played by education within this revolutionary strategy. In my opinion, this necessarily involves breaking away from some of the academic premises—in some cases abstract; in others, metaphysical—that maintain that there exists a body of rigid, closed concepts, which have been named a priori "revolutionary education." I would sincerely say, in relation to this science of education that has been proposed by the Soviets through their well-known manuals (the so-called Marxist pedagogy), that the problems of revolutionary pedagogy have been reduced to a body of abstract concepts that up to now have never offered us the possibility of a real intervention in the sphere of education. This idea may be a bit unexpected, and it has been expressed deliberately and in a slightly provocative sense. Naturally, I would like it if someone here would express the opposite point of view as regards this issue, but believe that there are real and concrete political problems that we have gone through in the university and that we are currently experiencing, in relation to this problem: either we propose a pedagogy of transition, situated in a concrete and historic temporal dimension, or else we must resort to an arsenal of rigid, closed, nontemporal concepts, such as those that we have received in these manuals.

There is another problem, or countless problems, in this same line of thought. I should like to establish a connection between Paulo Freire's words and the specific problematic that exists in the university today. I think that the proposals that have been made open up a perspective of intervention that has not always been evident: the possibility of a revolutionary education is not confined to the boundaries of a nonformal education; it is possible to elaborate an intervention program to change (and counterattack) the fundamental tendencies in formal education institutions toward the reproduction of the structures of domination.

This presents a series of operative problems. If Paulo Freire was able to collect his experiences in the field of nonformal education in order to formulate and theorize them in terms of a revolutionary pedagogy, this theoretical formulation immediately opened up, at least in a conceptual sense, a new universe of intervention—that of formal education. And yet, what is the program? What are the methods, the techniques, the procedures, by means of which the socialist or revolutionary forces, those who militate in the institutions education to bring about a revolutionary change in society, can carry out their work within these institutions?

Cultural Organizers

The problem acquires a much more relevant dimension in terms of the university or what would be the peak of the educational system, to the extent that if we follow Gramsci's thought, the role af the university is specifically that of the formation af intellectuals. And according to Gramsci, the role of intellectuals is that of cultural organizers, capable of intervening in the construction and practice of domination.

Intellectuals, as cultural organizers, would be a crucial and decisive component in the organization of a council, in the creation of domination. In consequence, revolutionary intervention in the university acquires a crucial, decisive, and fundamental significance.

How to act within the university? What type of intervention should be used? Is it possible to conceive a university for the formation of intellectuals, or not? Or, following Gramsci, organics of the working class, or in Freire's language, the popular masses. Is it possible to conceive and put into practice a program of this nature? It seems to me that these are some of the problems that arise from the proposal that Paulo Freire has made.

I think that at this moment we could open our dialogue to those of the audience who would like to intervene.

Conservative Utilization of Freirism?

E. Margolis: I would like to ask a question, a very old one, in my opinion, about Paulo Freire. I do not know to what extent you are familiar with the manner in which your language, your words, have been used in Mexico. My point of view is that Freire has been too institutionalized in Mexico; I mean, we even see that Freire's visits to Mexico have been organized on one hand by the INEA [Instituto Nacional de Educación para Adultos, National Institute for Adult Education], which is actually a quite bourgeois organism that is never going to allow a literacy campaign to reach all the Mexicans who need it; and on the other hand, the university is no longer popular, or never has been, according to many people. Those are Freire's visits to Mexico, and I am not talking about Nicaragua or Cuba, where Freire's method is used in a revolutionary manner and with a totally different perspective; therefore, my fear is that the more that Freire is used in Mexico, the more he is manipulated.

P. Freire: Look, in the 70s I tried to be intensely preoccupied with this problems at that time, it was closely associated with the word *conscientization*, and it was something incredible: wherever I went, I would find word associated with my project, which was, to a great extent, objectively reactionary, regardless of its sometimes being subjectively naive and sometimes clever. What I mean to say is that sometimes one is objectively reactionary, and yet, naively or cleverly so when one knows oneself to be reactionary. So, at that time I said to myself, there are only two ways to face this: the first is that what is the use of using the word *conscientization?* (And after 1987, you will no longer find the word *conscientization*; I participated in a seminar with Ivan Illich in Geneva, during which he once again used the concept of *descholarization* and I the concept of *conscientization*. It was there that I used this word for the last time. Naturally, I never abandoned the comprehension of the process which I had called conscientization, but I gave up the word).

The second thing that I had to do, and I think that I did in texts and in interviews, was to try to clarify and define the most naive and obscure concepts of my previous works that lent themselves to objectively reactionary uses of my ideas. I was also partly to blame for this. All of us, when we write, sometimes leave a margin for the misuse of what we say, and at that point I began to worry about this.

What has been happening since then is that I have been misused and misunderstood, especially by the right, and by the liberals too; and sometimes by some representatives of the left, who say, for example: "Paulo Freire is a serious intellectual, he is a man who is trying to make things over, but he has not as yet said that the class struggle is the moter of history." Therefore I say this, although when I say it I am not creating, but I must write. This is the magic of the written word. This the magic of the written word, which I reject.

Now, in relation to Mexico, obviously up to now there are two institutions that have brought me here, but I would come as well if any other institution invited me. One thing that people criticize me for, when I go to the United States, for example, is the fact that the universities sometimes charge a fortune to those who wish to participate in a seminar with me. I charge $500 or $600 for a weekend. But now I do something in the United States that I want to propose to you as well: I cannot pay my ticket to go abroad, although I probably earn a little more than some university professors, probably more than most university professors, because of the fact that receive some money for the books that I have written, but I cannot finance my own trips. So I always tell the groups who are interested in a more radical and popular discussion that they should take advantage of my visit, which has been paid for by those who have the money to pay for my ticket, my work, and my stay. In turn, I devote part of my visit, free of charge, to working with these other groups. For example, in the United States, I worked with ten groups that participate with the popular bases, without charging them anything; the universities paid my trip and on my part I gave approximately twenty days to those groups.

Elías Margolis speaks directly of the INEA; perhaps you are asking me why I came here on an invitation of the INEA, frankly admitting that my ideas could be or are distorted when put into practice. I came because for my ideas to be distorted, it was not necessary for me to be here; I have many examples of this, and in this place I was already being used, my name is already mentioned.

By coming here I thought that I would have the opportunity to answer to this in the intimacy of the institute, to say what I am now saying, and I actually did hold this discussion with all the groups. I came here twice, and besides holding these internal discussions with the groups, I publicly expressed my ideas. So, what happens is that you have two possibilities, the first is that your ideas are distorted, and you stay far away, with a "clean hands" attitude; you do not defend yourself, you do not get involved in certain politics, because you have to keep your hands clean—this, to me, is ethicism, moralism, but not moral. The second possibility is that you come and see how you are being restricted, to do this within the institution itself and clearly state what you think. You could tell me that it would be impossible, anyway, for the institute to do at least 70 percent of the things that I propose. Now, I ask you: could it be that from the starting point of a 20 percent, for example, of the use of a certain political space, you can or cannot perhaps expect to go any further than that 20 percent? If you refuse completely, you are adopting a position that is also respectable, but there is a risk involved. Both positions—that of accepting the 20 percent or that of refusing completely—involve a risk. In the first, you risk being even more restricted; in the second, you can still be restricted but without the possibility of saying that you are; you are limited without the possibility of protesting.

This is how I would answer, and I will also tell you something that I have learned through my personal experience: that there is only one way of not being restricted, and that is to do nothing, to stop doing. For example, I can imagine how many people from reading one's books end up doing exactly what one has not proposed, and yet say that they are doing it in one's name, because this does happen. What you have expressed seems absolutely legitimate to me, and more than that, I think that it is a political preoccupation that we should all share; we should be permanently measuring the spaces, the limits that we have, and the risks that we run.

But you were very right in saying that on one hand you run the risk of being recuperated, whether you come or not; on the other hand, there is no risk, but the joy of being "authenticated" by a revolution such as the one in Nicaragua. I am exposed to both situations, but anyway I thank for your great concern.

Reflections on the Revolution

B. Solares: Professor Freire: I understand that the problem that you have treated in your writings and in your talks is the problem of the revolution, that is, you are making a proposal as to how we are going to make a revolution from the starting paint of the democratization of education.

P. Freire: No, I do not think that pedagogic practice could do that; however, in the process of the proposal, the problem consists of how to make the revolution, or how we are going to carry it out.

B. Solares: In the way that your concept of education has been developed, I find it very closely realted to the manner in which Marx develops the concept of education in the Thesis, understanding it as a political education, and also understanding that this concept of political education is highly developed by Marcuse in the '60s, especially in his text on revolution, in which he explains education as a process in the institutions fundamentally, through which we advance and from which we acquire the conceptions of everything that we seek.

For me it is very important to keep in mind the time in which Marcuse was situated—precisely in the '60s—when on one hand, apparently after an experience of the workers' movement, based on social-democratic participation, and on the other hand, all the stabilization process, new alternatives for change were proposed, alternatives that are above all external to the directly productive process. The movements appear in feminism, in proletarianism, in the universities; but it seems that the revolution or the revolutionary subject mentioned earlier, is a subject that is no longer proletarian, but another kind of subject, one who is, once again, outside of the productive process. Besides, this new subject even doubts Marxism, especially when the labor movement is once again immersed in the capitalistic process, which absorbs it and provides benefits. At the same time, Marxism is discredited among the socialists, and no longer seems to be the strategic weapon that Marx thought could be used for the subject's liberation; it is just another theory. I am concerned about the same thing in the discourse as Elías. It may well be a discourse in which the problem of the revolution is posed; it can be used either by representatives of the bourgeoisie or by a school where the goal is the reproduction in society. At the same time, it can be a discourse that provokes enthusiasm toward working in a literacy campaign or that encourages the Latin American socialist revolutions, because this discourse can be so ambivalent that it may be used in one way or another. While reading one of your books [*Pedagogy of the Oppressed*], I tried to see exactly what the essence of the discourse was, to see what exactly was the essence of the revolution that you were proposing, in order to find out why it could be used by one tendency or another, mutually antagonistic. And the problem that I found was that this pedagogic theory of the oppressed that you have elaborated is difficult to apply, precisely because this student-educator, this feedback that you propose, would require many conditions to actually be put into practice. I mean, to the extent to which the student is an alienated subject, as you also postulate in your books, it is difficult for this same alienated subject to start the revolution.

Marx also had this problem—that is, when he proposes the proletariat as the subject of the revolution, but a subject constantly absorbed within the capitalist process.

A Liberating Education

This would be my first version; the second is that I am aware that education can be understood in two ways: either as an education for the reproduction of the system, which is the one that is practiced in the contemporary system of education; and on the other hand, the education that you propose, a liberating education. The problem that presents itself to the pedagogues is how to practice a liberating education within institutions that have oppression, and not liberation, as an objective. In addition, in order to confront the problem of education for liberation, these pedagogues do not necessarily have to prepare their students for the work process, but rather on the fringe of this process, in their criticism toward that work process.

Therefore I ask myself if you would accept that pedagogy, as you practice it, has a limited or restricted sense.

P. Freire: But of course, I think that I said that during the first part of the morning session. We would rather be speaking then of an education which goes beyond these limits outside of the institutions, in other fields, so to speak. I also said this in *La Pedagogia del Oprimido*, when I spoke about work outside of the system.

In the first place, it seems to me that you have very well expressed what you meant to says you work in the School of Political Science, and you asked a question about things that I said this morning, the question of how to direct your work toward nonreproduction of the dominating ideology within an institution that has been created for its reproduction. I would answer your question with another one: is it possible that you are reproducing the dominant ideology here, doing what you just did from within the university itself? Is it possible that this morning, a morning of reproduction of the dominant ideology, could be a challenge to that reproduction, and yet, be taking place in the university? With this I am not trying to say that the dominating class is good, not but only that these are the limits of power. If power face-to-face with those who have no power were so annihilating, then there would not even be the possibility of speaking about power, because there would be nothing to counteract power and power itself would not be known.

What you do, and I hope that you do very well, in the School of Political Science, what the professors who are here do, is exactly what I say we should do. What we are trying to do, with all the restrictions that really exist, all that we are trying to do is to swim against the tide. But what to me would be terrible is if we said: since what I can do by swimming against the tide is very little, then I am going over to the other side, and I am going to reproduce, because it is easier. That would be much more than cynicism.

There is no need to resign from the university; you can imagine what it means now to try to resign, to get out of here, if you have to keep on surviving. So, I do not suggest that anyone here hand in his or her resignation. On the contrary, we must occupy the spaces and fill them up. For this reason, I always suggest that in order to more or less fulfill a minimum part of our task well, we should do something that I call "ideological materialing of the institutional space." We need to know who we can count on in the total space, which here is very large; we need to know who we cannot count on, we must know where our enemies within the institution are. Who are those people that are watching us to catch us in any mistake; we need to know exactly who we can count on to join forces and produce more, and be better.

But in your question the issue arises of how to work against the reproduction of ideology in an institution created for this purpose. Obviously, and you also said it, within an institution such as this neither we nor the students are necessarily close to the productive process. But we can reach the productive act as the objective of our reflection, in the same way that you reach behavior as a scientific exception, that you reach a part of the political history of Mexico, and in that piece of the political and social history of Mexico, you understand that pedagogy is present; why should we not understand the productive act while teaching politics, for example? Why not study with the students about how for the bourgeois class it is fundamental not to reveal the productive process just as it occurs in a capitalist economy. I remember Braverman's assertion [Harry Braverman (1982). The degradation of work in the twentieth century. *Monthly Review*, 34 (1):1–13.]; he uses a phrase that is quite dramatic: "The more science interferes or is incorporated into the productive process, the less knowledge the working class has." This is the truth; a few years ago there was a myth that in an advanced capitalist economy, there would have to be more training in scientific knowledge for the dominated class. This is a myth; today it has been proven that in the most advanced capitalist society, specialized workers are trained in three hours, three-hour courses, to do precisely the minimum in a production line, changing from one to another.

Popular Culture and Alienation

I think this is a problem that we have all faced; nevertheless, it is necessary for the left-wing intellectual to know, not just by reading a book, but by conviction acquired in practice, that the less rigorous level of knowledge on which we find the working class has nothing to do with the nonexistent ontology of this class.

By this I mean to say that the level or levels of popular wisdom cannot be explained metaphysically, but historically and socially; I do not hold the working class and the popular classes responsible for incompetence, as if we could say: as intellectuals, we know, and the working classes do not know because they cannot.

We sometimes have practices that reveal these metaphysics, which are absolutely false. What Marx proposed was not this; Marx knew that in the structures of a capitalist bourgeois society, the workers' education is one that reproduces them as workers in said society, and the education of the bourgeois is one that reproduces him as dominant. We must, therefore, have the conviction that the levels of alienation, the levels of less rigorous knowledge, are a result of the social, political, economical, and cultural level on which the working classes are to be found.

These concretely constituted levels of knowledge are precisely our starting point in working with the popular classes in order for them to improve the level at which they are at present, for reasons imposed by the bourgeoisie. This means that the working classes must take their own alienation in their hands, questioning themselves about alienation. By this I am proposing an academy in which the starting point shall be the level at which the working classes are to be found, and not our own.

The "Here" of the Students

One of our greatest mistakes as educators and politicians is not perceiving that our "here" is the student's and the people's "there." Of course there are exceptions! There are professors who are "here," and it is not yet even the student's "here"; this happens because we forget our "here" of before, and we forget that any "there" implies movement, and that any movement contains "historicity."

There is no static movement; that would be a contradiction of the very concept. The "here" of the popular classes is precisely the starting point from which they must advance toward a different "there," and it may be that set of certainties, quite uncertain in my opinion, of the revolution. And when we forget all this, the only path left, is that of authoritarianism. There is also a risk when we accept this as the truth, and that is the risk of lapsing into "spontaneism," which is fatal from the political point of view, and then the issue is not to leave the masses to their own rhythm, nor to start off from the masses or try to make them set out from the point where I am, but to set out with them, so to speak.

The intellectual must walk again down a road that he or she has already traveled, and this is something beautiful, to travel again a familiar road, and there is no possibility of doing or learning something with those who are doing it for the first time. To use a very technical expression, I say that to the extent that the educator undertakes this long walk, inasmuch as the student or the popular masses are developing or putting into practice their "cognoscibility," the educator is remaking his or her "cognoscibility" through the "cognoscibility" of the students. It is precisely the cognitive exercise of the students that compels me to remake my own "cognoscibility." In my opinion, this is what has to be done, and of course this implies one of the functions of the revolution, which is not authoritarian but it is not liberal, either. Politics are difficult.

The Uncertainty of Liberating Education

G. Villaseñor: Perhaps what I am going to say is slightly out of context, but there is an uncertainty that I have had for some time, an uncertainty that I think is shared to some extent by many of us who are working in higher education: how to concentrate concrete forms for higher education to become a liberating education. There must be many theoretical problems involved in this proposal, but we will not go into them at this moment, since I do not even have them systematically classified. We are dealing here with a problem of a completely practical nature. I think that at least for some of the people present here that I know, there exists a concern that higher education in practice be an education that contributes to change. I also believe that we are all quite aware that the space of higher education is small, and that it is not "the lever," as Freire has pointed out.

On the other hand, the concrete circumstances of our country indicate that we going through a very peculiar situation. Although I have no doubt that on the wide road of history, we are slowly advancing towards a social change that will lead us to a socialist society, I also believe that in this journey there are pauses and that at this moment, in the concrete situation of our country and its higher education, we are at such a point, during which it would seem that we have taken a step backward. I am convinced that we have reached such a point, as you can see by the general policies toward higher education; we are at a moment not of advancing, but of involution. There is currently an attempt to use higher education as a practical element, not for advancing toward social change, but instead as a way to affirm a regression. I do not know how much this opinion may be shared, or if it is shared by many of those who are present. But in the face of these policies, even though one searching for concrete forms for things to be otherwise, one feels the imposition of force, and one feels as well a weakness, an inability to imagine the means by which higher education could be liberating.

This came to my mind because of what Gilberto Guevara was saying when he referred to formal education as a possible contribution to change. I would like to ask Paulo Freire if in his experience as an educator, in which he undoubtedly must have encountered circumstances similar to those that he described, perhaps he could point out some topics, some basic and general factors of higher education, which we should try to influence with certain concrete tactics, in order to truly convert higher education into an element of transformation. There are things that I suppose are more or less generalized in higher education, and this is what I am referring to, because the concrete historical application of the immediate tactics would have to be something that we ourselves would do. But I would like to ask if we can detect some basic factors of influence in higher education on which tactics should be tried out in order to materialize the possible dream.

P. Freire: I think that Gilberto can elaborate on this subject. There is no doubt in my mind that today one of the characteristics of international bourgeoisie in the capitalist systems, be they highly developed or similar to ours, is a more authoritarian attitude, which is evident in the reproducing role of dominant ideology.

I think that it is not so important to ask ourselves, Could education at the university level be like this? but rather, Is it possible that we, in a political perspective of transformation, will be able to use to our advantage the university space created by society? That would be the question, because we are only asking, Is it possible that university education could propose a new form of education? I think not, because this would be equivalent to asking the dominating class if it is planning a type of education that would rebel against its domination. Naturally, it would have to say no, because up to now there has never been a dominating class in history that committed suicide, and there is no reason to expect that this should occur in Latin America. It seems to me that the question of interest to us is, Will we, or will we not have the possibility of taking full advantage of the spaces—we as doctors, biologists, chemists, physicists, political scientists, psychologists, etc.? I think that we should hold private congresses, without microphones, without intervies, without the press or anything like that; congresses for ourselves alone, in order to discuss what we can do, and I think that we can do many things. Because if it were not possible to do something, I should ask how it is that the university, as bad as it is and as a reproducer of the dominant ideology, has allowed us to escape such as we are. Perhaps we are geniuses, the chosen of God; no, of course not! We had an experience outside of the university, a social practice that reeducated us.

Educational Nihilism

G. Guevara-Niebla: Going back to what Paulo was saying, I believe that in order to have a truly revolutionary change within the institution, regardless of the proportions of this change, there must necessarily be a convergence of favourable historical and social conditions on one hand, and on the other, there must be a human element of volition, a social force capable of becoming the subject of change. I think that the element of *will* that Freire is emphasizing is very important in any serious thought regarding education and schools in Mexico, which in my opinion, has been weighed down by very pessimistic conceptions.

I want to go back to the historic time of radical education, during the '30s—socialist education, through which Mexico experienced enormous optimism and which implicated a great social mobilization that has few parallels in Latin America. On the other hand, I think that the radicalization and the disintegration of the student milieu after 1968 coincided with the intervention of certain conceptions that spread a pessimistic outlook which annulled the component of will, and I think that this outlook still influences our way of thinking about the problems of education and particularly higher education. Thus this type of impersonal positions in relation to the evolution of the institutions, and thus the rejection of the institution, which in the end leads to immobility and to an enormous political passivity. In other words, the discussion that came up as to whether the institutions had been created for one thing or for another involves a fundamental debate about the nature of social institutions. In our country, we have hardly discussed the nature of educational institutions. Are these institutions a reflection or a creation of a single will, that of the dominating class? Can we sum up the state in its totality, or the entirety of state institutions in a single will, in a unique and unified wish or aspiration? Are the institutions simple reflections of the economy?

I think that these questions have been dominated by fatalistic answers, and that these positions have lead us to a standstill, to a passiveness where the component of volition is suppressed to give way to pessimistic positions. We need an important injection of optimism. Practice has revealed that these abstract, fatalistic conceptions of the institutions are false; Freire was referring to the nature of this encounter, to the fact that it is taking place in a university ambience. But this reunion is no more than a minor element among more significant historic facts that could not be denied—for example, the simple fact that socialist opposition in this country, made up of a number of important political organizations, is an opposition that has historically developed within the university. It would be very difficult to contradict this statement. In any case, we could discuss and analyze the cultural and professional fields one-by-one, and we would see how the intellectual forces that act within the university, have struggled, sometimes with surprising success, to create alternate forms of theorizing and practicing their professions.

At this moment, there exists a wide universe of professional fields in this country. I would just like to point

out what is happening today in the field of medicine in Mexico; what is happening in architecture, and all the important ideas that are being developed around the concepts of popular housing, of urbanism, of urban development, etc. Consider as well what is happening in science itself, with the questioning of *scientificism* which has been taking place in the basic sciences. In literature, even in sophisticated fields such as literature and arts, there are also new forms of culture beginning to appear, which naturally have not yet matured sufficiently, but neither have they found as yet a political leadership program that serves as a vehicle. The socialist forces in Mexico have historically paid little attention to the cultural front. Instead, there has been a strong inheritance of anti-intellectualism among the socialist forces, an important inheritance of Jacobinism and authoritarianism.

Therefore, we must settle our accounts with our past experience, and with an inherited way of understanding ideologies, so that we may inject new strength into our struggle or into any intervention, any action, towards generating a higher education with the objective not of oppression, but of liberation, generically directed toward the creation of a democratic and liberating education.

It seems to me that we could delve further into the instrumental part, but this would be more complicated. I think that today, it is possible to talk about the programs that should be established in the field of history, the field of agriculture, etc.

Authentic Education

Another doubt that was brought up by what Paulo said, that I thought of asking him about and forgot at the appropriate moment, was in relation to the *national*

dimension of the problems involved in education and those of the revolution. What is the program? What are the national specifications of a pedagogical program of transition? What is the influence of our national specificity when dealing with these subjects? For one thing, it is not possible to use, without mediation, certain categories that originate in advanced, metropolitan countries—for example, the concept of alienation proposed by Marcuse. And then Blanca introduced another relevant problem, that of the relation between education and production, and he mentioned something important, in asking to what extent liberating education is in the end constricted, compelled, forced to accept that it must form productive abilities, and that finally, one way or the other, any form of education is linked to certain production plans. Blanca asked how we can liberate if we preserve this link that enslaves us to certain forms of production; this problem seems to have a specific dimension in the United States and it must have a different one here.

P. Freire: In regard to your question, in the first place think that it is absolutely fundamental that we (and this is probably a specificity, that we can ask about this) as educators, as professors, should be able to offer a theoretical contribution to a revolutionary practice outside of the university, because obviously the university cannot be the vanguard of any revolution; this is not the nature of the institution. The same is true for the church.

In trying to answer your question, we are necessarily led to other questions: among them, one belonging to the field of epistemology, which means that we are asking ourselves about science, about scientific precision, what is exactness, what is science, what is scientific knowledge.

Besides, we do not have only one epistemology; we have different approaches that explain what knowledge is and how it is acquired.

I believe that you who are in the university possess the intellectual, personal, and physical conditions to create now, if you have not already done so, a group that obviously should have the same political position, a multidisciplinarian group. Far example, I think that a physicist-mathematician who studies quantum physics could make an interesting contribution to the discussion of the role of subjectivity. A biologist has a great deal to do with any reflections on the art of knowing, on the biological alienation of knowledge, of the need originated by research. The same could be said of mathematicians, epistemologists, pedagogues, social scientists, etc., who can contribute to any serious thinking, for example, about those two moments of the act of knowing that we could call in academic terms the "nonbiological circle"—the moment in which the knowledge that has already been produced comes to be known, and the moment in which one creates or produces the knowledge that had not up to then been produced. In fact, there exist only these two moments in the biological cycle: either you come to know that which is already known, or you create that which is not yet known, but these two moments are of a great epistemologic, pedagogic, and political importance.

The Dichotomy of These Two Moments

It is antidialectic, antiepistemologic, and antinatural; when these two moments are separated, the task of education, no matter at what level, becomes a kind of space in which "knowledge" is sold, and the professor is no longer a specialist, but a salesman of knowledge.

In practicality, this means that established knowledge is received, transmitted from those who possess it to those who do not possess it. This is one of the consequences of the dichotomy between coming to know knowledge that already exists and creating the new knowledge. In facts the creation of knowledge that does not exist and the act of learning that which already exists require that there be cognitive subjects, an educator and a student, a series of fundamental attitudes that have to do with a liberating testimony.

One of the qualities or virtues that we must incorporate is that of curiosity; I wonder how it would be possible to come to know, without curiosity. Another virtue is that of moving, changing, acting. The epistemology of Piaget is profoundly rich in dialectics, for there is no knowledge outside of transformation; I transform and come to know through the process of transformation, and the farther away that I get after the whole process of transformation, theoretically the more I appropriate my own transformation, which I accepted. Therefore, participation is a virtue without which knowledge cannot be obtained. These two fundamental qualities are annulled by us when we restrict ourselves to simply transmitting knowledge. There is no need to be curious in order to transcribe transference; we must be passive, we must have good behavior. This is why reading, as the act of rewriting that which is read, is something that is not generally done. To read and to rewrite what one reads, and not just memorize mechanically what has been read—there are many professors who suggest three hundred books to be read in one semester, when I doubt that they have done so themselves. Mao Tse-tung said something marvelous: "I greatly fear the intellectual who reads only one book a year." There are people who think that to read is to stroll over the words, and it is not so. To read is a form of entering into the discourse in order to understand it from within; it is to establish the relation between text and context, it is to discover that which in the text is historical, set in the context that generates it as well.

Four Reflections on Educational Distortion

J. Pescador O.: I would like to make a few observations about the subjects that we have been discussing this morning. The first one is that we should examine the facts to see if we are not so involved in the educational process that we may be forgetting some factors that to some extent determine it, and sometimes even preshape it with respect to what we want to do. When Freire was talking about a series of experiences and concrete actions in response to Guillermo Villaseñor's intervention—the nonseparation of teaching and research, the need for multidisciplinarian work groups, the teaching of critical reading—we recalled that these have been postulated and used in one way or another in education for many years. Now we must ask ourselves why this is so, why, if these principles are being confirmed through many experiences, they have always resulted in failure, not only in universities, but at any level of education. What comes to my mind as an answer is that the co-optation of men to which Freire referred also may apply to ideas and to institutions. The curriculum of basic education is full of words such as *curiosity, creativity, discovery.* But there is no possibility of promoting these behaviors and attitudes. Said curriculum has existed for ten years in Mexico and it is full of these kind of concepts. The same thing occurs with the notion that we could call "new epistemology" or "alternative epistemology." In Latin America, there have been many advances in this concept, with references to science and to popular culture, but my fear is that now UNESCO, too, has appropriated these terms and has practically incorporated them into its international language, the same as it did with the concept of *participative research*, which also originated precisely within our geographical boundaries. My second reflection has to do with the real possibility of transforming the institutions of higher education. Is it going to be by means of their practice, by that of the curriculum, or is it going to be through their links with the external environment, which seems to absorb the institution of education?

Each day we advance with a greater vigor toward scholarization, even though a few years ago, precisely due to Ivan Illich's arguments, there was the belief that to descholarize was an alternative in order to be able to advance toward revolutionary change, thus freeing ourselves from that which operated in the opposite way. In spite of what has been said here, I think that there still exists, for the great majorities, an enormous optimism toward the institution of education, and that this is an angle that must be analyzed in order to determine if the convenient thing is to continue supporting this demand for more education, without a critical sense, or to go back to the starting points of fifteen years ago.

My third reflection has to do with the great changes that have occurred in Latin America in the field of social sciences. We advance in economic and social theory when dependency is postulated as a form of explaining the relationship between the developed and underdeveloped countries; we advance in political science when the concepts of the state and the theories of the state are incorporated in order to explain the function fulfilled by it in underdeveloped countries. We advance in education, and we have with us precisely one of the representatives of this concept of a liberating education; anthropology, too, is one of the fields of notable achievements in terms of research and what has happened in the last twenty years? All these changes have been incorporated as a language into the system of the dominating ideology, and little has been done to advance on those postulates that seemed to point toward a different change, at least in the conception of social sciences. This situation is cause for concern, and with this I go on to the fourth reflection. For example, Paulo Freire became known in Mexico after the translation of his books from English. Strangely enough, his book *Pedagogy of the Oppressed*, as I understand, was first printed in English when his theses were being compared with those of Ivan Illich. To a great extent, this may be explained by the greater availability of the means that exist in the industrialized countries to accelerate and facilitate the co-opting to which we have referred. I think that this would be a very adventurous. hypothesis, but one has the impression that this stage of changes, which pointed in the right direction to make a new strategy of development possible or viable, was not only stopped, but suffered a retrogression, as Guillermo said just now, and we returned to more and more conservative positions.

Concretely in the case of education, instead of still thinking of questioning the educational apparatus, we suddenly accept the idea that what we must do is expand the educational system, perhaps because the idea exists in Latin America that popular education may be an alternative. Nonetheless, the curious thing is that this form of understanding education as popular education, as the education that is demanded by the groups of working classes, of the majority classes, is also already being incorporated into the political and ideological mechanism of the dominant groups. The case of the literacy campaign that we mentioned here is useful to illustrate our argument, since today two ways of looking at this coexist, speaking in a dichotomous sense: one traditional, and one with a social concern. What is happening now? One exists, and I believe that the mention of the INEA was quite clear; it assumes, internalizes, and appropriates the idea of a liberating education, but with many limitations, with a method that is not even Freirian and that they call "the generating word."

I am afraid that exactly the same thing could happen to the concept of popular education; that is, the co-optation of its liberating potential and its "fitting" to a social demand.

The universities have also defined alternative projects which have been incorporated into institutionality by financial and political pressures. To this, we must add the fact that for the dominating group, there are other means, other very effective alternatives that allow them to calmly observe this movement of greater freedom in the educational institutions. I am referring concretely to the world of work and to that of the communication media. Thus any alternative in education should incorporate, in the clearest manner possible, these two concepts: in the first place, because in the working world the whole process of liberation may be reverted, except perhaps this permanently reflexive form of reading the texts; and in the second place, because the media have become a very promising form of imposing hegemony, to legitimate an order of things and even to widen, as the reproducers that they are, the ideology of the dominating class.

Alternative Education

P. Freire: I am afraid that exactly the same thing can happen to the concept of popular education; what is happening now is that to some extent, when these ideas are incorporated, a restriction is imposed not only on people, but also on institutions, as is the case with the universities.

There exists the alternative of thinking of pedagogy not as the agent of transformation but as a means, a space, which must be used to advantage and which should be widened. I have the impression that we would be late the reinvention of power, because this power is being reinvented at this moment by the dominating class, and in consequence, the reinvention should not be looked at in the long run, but rather as a daily action, incorporating new elements into this pedagogical definition that has been proposed.

I find that the intervention of José Angel Pescador was excellent. I would even like to say to you, in all sincerity, that this seminar has been for me the most interesting in more than ten years, and I ask myself if I have been more or less at the high level required by this seminar.

I agree absolutely with the analytic, critical discourse of Pescador, and yet I would like to say that we, from the position that we have assumed, could never be taken by surprise in relation to the restrictive power of the dominant class. We cannot enter into the struggle for the transformation of society ignoring the fact that the dominant class has an extraordinary power to "forklorize" the most advanced ideas.

If we enter into the struggle without being convinced that this is what happens, we are simply doing harm to ourselves. We must expect the curricula to stimulate curiosity, a critical spirit, and democratic participation, but the contrary occurs. We must create curiosity and participation; even when the dominant class states in its written discourse that curiosity must be stimulated, that the critical and creative aspects of the children must be stimulated, it does this in a restricting manner.

The Revolution Is Loving

For me, the point is not to stop using words such as *curiosity* or *creativity*, only because the dominating class has started to use them; I also think that it is absurd to stop using the word *love*. There is no revolution without love; the revolution is loving; The fact that the bourgeoisie has distorted an important word has nothing to do with me. My struggle has to do precisely with restoring their meaning to words. It is by living curiosity with the students that I defend curiosity, and not by talking about curiosity without being curious, because there are many noncurious ways of talking about curiosity, such as the authoritarian way, for example.

2

Curriculum and Social Reality

Introduction

M. Escobar: The subject today is curriculum and society, but Paulo has proposed to take into account something that remained pending from yesterday, so we can continue with the analysis of the relation between education and power. And for this reason Alfredo Fernández, who will be the moderator for this subject, has prepared an introductory summary so that the continuity with yesterday's theme is not lost.

A. Fernández: With the purpose of continuing with yesterday's theme, I will provide a brief summary of what was discussed; I will especially stress the main points. I am conscious that many of them will not be mentioned in this abstract; nevertheless, I will deal with those that serve mainly to continue the discussion of education and politics and in some way relate them to the problem of the curriculum with its power in society.

Summary of the Discussion of Education and Power

Actually, in Paulo's work it is difficult to differentiate between the political problem and the problem of knowledge on the one hand, and that of the role of the intellectuals on the other. These articulate themselves theoretically and practically in a totality. For the analytical objectives of this seminar, I have tried to consider them separately.

The main subjects discussed yesterday were the following: an approximation of the concept of social revolution and change evidently not reaching a concept of change or of revolution. It was said that these are basic categories for explaining the role of education for self-reliance.

The idea of a pedagogical relation such as the relation to power was introduced and consequently reference was made to the universal concept as a form of obtaining a pedagogical revolutionary relation. Paulo rejected pedagogism as an ultimate expression of educational practice and said that he has criticized it all through his educational practice as a pedagogue, but always been conscious of the difference, even if he was not very explicit in his initial work. In fact, his educational practice was always related to his political practice.

Paulo spoke about educational reproduction and here he differentiated dialectically between the reproduction work of the dominant class and the "production work," or as he himself called it the "reproduction of an liberating education 'produced' by ourselves." Paulo emphasized that the "reproduction" and the "production" are two axes on which an educational act is built and rebuilt. He further stressed that our strategic purpose, as he called it, "the possible dream," cannot be obtained through domestication. Here he indicated the importance of the congruency between the means and objectives by which he confirmed that the revolution is also pedagogical. Nevertheless, he warned that education is not and will not be the lever of the revolution.

With this in mind, it should remain very clear that in Paulo's work, politics are not a separate sphere of education but rather, the political content that education possesses has an intrinsically pedagogical character. Education does not possess a political dimension but is in fact political.

The Symbols of Power

The subject of education and power will provide an opening for our discussion today. The first part of our discussion will deal with the symbolic structure of power. It has been stated that the dominating class, through its hegemony in this structure, recuperates the liberating concepts of education and immediately transforms them into empty terminology, void of useful meanings and strength as ideas. To illustrate the above, some examples will be mentioned concerning the curriculum of basic education in Mexico, allegedly based on the concepts of curiosity, creativity, and criticism; these have, however, become only words. But Paulo pointed out that these words always lack the expected content; they await the re-creation of their content through the political practice of liberating education. At this point Paulo continued the discussion and reflection on the social generation of pedagogical concepts.

P. Freire: I would add something else on this point. I remember that José Angel Pescador's analysis of this subject was discussed. I believe that one of our tasks in this struggle is to obtain power at a symbolic level. I think that this struggle is permanent, since it proves that those concepts slacken sometimes with defined purposes and sometimes without any explicit intention, in the school programming, in pedagogical practice. Now then, if I take yesterday's word as an example of the concept of curiosity, it simply appears "written on paper," ignored in the practice. For this reason I am not interested in succumbing to the temptation of reading another word since it too would be limited; what I do care about is to question whether I accept that curiosity is fundamental or not. If I accept that it is, then I would try to experience it with the students, and on living this with them, I would state the process itself in which the word is "depleted." Declaring the process of depletion by limitation principally means living the declaration and not only speaking of it.

Curiculum and Conceptual Wear-and-Tear

P. Freire: I have spoken on the subject of curiosity, but I could elaborate a long list of words or concepts that have been "depleted." In fact, it would be good if we carried out a type of investigation among ourselves on the groups of concepts that have been depleted, in order to experience them and revive them, really putting them in practice. I feel that curiosity sometimes coexists in several of us, although we may have progressive and radical political opinions, in a strange manner coincide with the vigor of authoritarianism. I do not know if you observe these phenomena here in Mexico, but they exist in Brazil. There is certainly a mistrust of every live, more democratic, more open work procedure that seems to go against the strict scientific academy. In this sense there's a tendency to consider some colleagues spontaneous and allied with a progressive (I do not want to call it revolutionary since I have a great respect for the meaning of the word—it's grand!) position for the simple reason that they work together with the students and are set on stimulating their creativity. Nevertheless, such colleagues are considered manipulators. This creates a dilemma—manipulation and spontaneity—difficult to solve. I do not accept either positions; I usually lean toward the concept of radical democracy, which I feel is opposed to these two. In the two positions that are criticized I think that there is no creativity, no seriousness, no curiosity but there is oppression of the students' ability to think and create. The curricular concept is derived from this attitude and the curriculum is represented as a type of unintentional perversity that would popularly be expressed in the following phrase: "Let me see what it is like, so I can see what it will be like." And so the curriculum is elaborated in an absolute, wanton manner and not in an anarchistic form. From this point of view, the curriculum will appear as a mercenary, hired to save those who will remain under domestication. This is incredible! The authoritarian solutions in this mercenary sense of those who organize them, present curriculum that receives from God the task of saving the poor devils.

I feel that our effort should be a creative effort. Of course we will have all the imaginable limits in the task of creating and re-creating the curricular reality. Nobody doubts that numerous difficulties exist that put obstacles in the path of creative possibility; nevertheless, I firmly believe that one of our tasks is precisely to discuss with the students the obstacles to creativity.

I do not want to reduce all this to mere intellectual comprehension, but it is absolutely indispensable that there exist certain critical reflection and theory on the practice of creating curriculum where obstacles are found in relation to the determined limits of authoritarian power. It is absolutely fundamental to understand the nature of the limits of creative praxis for this. (I would like to stop here and offer the floor to other colleagues who would like to delve deeper into the subject.)

A. Fernández: At this moment it would be convenient to continue discussing the meaning of the symbolic structure of power—the forms of reproduction, the development and updating of domination—and from there to analyze, paraphrasing the Freirian concepts, how the symbolic structure starts the process of building, of generating, the new "words of domination."

G. Guevara-Niebla: Well, I see a dilemma here with the opposite opinions in relation to the symbolic order, because I think that Paulo has spoken of two alternatives in relation to the word. At one point, he indicated that his effort was directed toward recuperating the meanings, reintegrating the symbol with its meaning. And now when he is speaking to us about the limitations, the alienation, of the word on the part of the power, one asks if the problem resides precisely in the separation of the symbol from its meaning or in the fact that the symbol of the word and the meaning are essentially alienated because of power. So this suggests that in reality we have before us two different educational strategies with this differentiation. Or that we conceive of culture as a unit that can momentarily be vulnerable because of separation or strains between the symbol and the meaning. Or that we conceive of culture as two opposed symbolic orders. At the same time, this would give us two different tasks: we would unite symbols and meanings; or we would make an effort to provide new words, alternative words—in other words, to develop an alternative symbolic order. I think that Paulo has an interesting point, but although it is historically and socially possible to live the meaning of the symbol, depleted because of limitations imposed by power think that it is also fundamental to accept that there is a problem in relation to the limitation of power that the domination has over the order itself, over the denied symbolic forms and over the cultural forms of the subordinate social classes. This is a problem that was stated yesterday by José Angel Pescador very clearly. Or more precisely, he pronounced it very clearly without it having been the main point of his contributions. We now have a group of questions that serves to broaden the explanation of these phenomena, such as: Why the limitations? How do we understand state limitations? and also, What is choice sharing? How is it developed? Understanding limitation and choice sharing depend on how we understand the state. To me it seems that in Mexico, current theories in education seem to be supported by the socialist and revolutionary group force. It is the conception of a monolithic state—in other words, the conception of a unitary subject provided with clear will and determination. For example, if the workers' movement struggles because it believes in schools for the workers, and the state creates the schools, this unitary vision of the state would be interpreted as choice sharing with the state itself; the state therefore, limited, alienated, the demand of the workers. It is worth asking ourselves if we need to understand the state as an entity or as a domain that reflects in some way the relation of the social forces. I do not think that these two opinions or conceptions of the state's political power will allow us to determine our role in the preceding two strategies.

P. Freire: Deep down, I think that the space where the limitations are given is an ideological, very concrete domain and it is given in a relation that is sometimes not clear but provides exactly the relation between Power in power and the need to create a new power on the part of those who do not have it. I think that this is the domain where limitation flourishes and not the other.

In order to confront the Power, the popular forces need to gain power (real or symbolic) to preserve or re-create it and thereby obtain power with which a new type of society will be established. These popular forces that do not have power have to understand their own struggle, their own action, theoretically. They have to establish their militant tactics; they have to consider clearly consider what will be the domains of struggle. They should, for this reason, develop an interpretive theoretical statement of the situation in which power is in search of power. In the meantime, the Power is in power, it has to preserve its power. That is, it has to preserve itself in power (and this is not a play on words) and Power in power has a few mechanisms at its disposal—the power of symbolic combination and not only power by physical force.

In the symbolic effort, the Power in power has domination as one of its instruments—by means of imposing limitations and depleting the symbolic forces that emerge from the popular classes in search for power. It is interesting to observe how this comes about. This is a question of struggling for power and it is not possible to conceive that education was the speech of power. In this manner, the basic understanding of education, of educational practice, of the curricular question, of programmatic content are linked to the arenas of political confrontation or to the relation with the power that establishes itself. In the long run, understanding the confrontation between power that is trying to remain and the forces that struggle for a new power helps us obtain a more critical comprehension of the curriculum. Know-ing the logic of the symbolic power will therefore allow the designers of curricula to avoid taking the indexes from books imported from the U.S.A. and using them to establish a study program. The other critical option consists for me in understanding social reality, what goes on in our "world." It is not unusual in university education for us to train students to read textbooks, sometimes very efficiently, but these books are not really read, because there exists a dichotomy between the text and the context. In this way the university dedicates its abstract task and appears as a type of sacred temple where to be chaste is a virtue.

The chastity of university, but not academic, knowledge probably hinders us greatly in understanding reality. For example, I believe that many of us have difficulty in understanding the daily newspapers. We also do not have good social intercourse with the television, we do not fight with the news programs on T V., we are receptors without thoughts; we only listen. Everything seems to be so far away that the nature of the relation of power is hidden from us. I do not know if I am now lost in that constellation of things that you (Gilberto) argued. But I do think that when you brought it up I found one of great importance. I think that it is possible that in the confrontation between the search of power and the preservation of existing power, it is tactically fundamental for us to give life to our ideas—force or words—like I did with the word *consciousness*. That dialectic has a lot to do with the rationale of the revolutionary strategy and only makes sense to those who can understand the revolutionary change in a less catastrophic and insurrectionist manner and also for those who conceive of the revolutionary change as a democratic change, with the active participation of the masses, where the modifications of the subjectivity play a definite role. On one hand I remember an excellent statement made by Amilcar Cabral, who said that the struggle for liberation is a political act with probable moments of being up in arms.

That is the question! and there are still those who indicate the contrary: "The struggle for liberation is an armed struggle with any or no political moment." When this happens, the revolutionaries do not understand the extraordinary political and armed moment, and they reduce every armed moment to a moment of military tactics. On one of my visits to Granada, I remember that I held private but very open talks with Bishop and with the minister of education (who was also assassinated) lasting more than four hours. Bishop asked me to hold a specific conversation with groups of the armed forces and in speaking with them, I quoted exactly what Amilcar thought of the militancy and I told them, "In my judgment, if instead of accepting Amilcar's suggestions, that is to say if instead of thinking about militants you become military, we will have a coup sooner or later in the state of Granada, and I went on to say, "One must be a political militant with weapons in one's hands, not just a simple soldier devoid of politics. It is sad now to accept that militarism has turned to militancy. I think that these elements are both ideological within the same horizon of the revolution. The revolutionary concepts are always dichotomized. Consider for example, a revolution composed by cadres and a revolution of the masses. The necessary cadres will never be able to separate from the masses; on the contrary, they should be considered permanently with the masses. And this is where we find the pedagogical nature of the political act: the masses and the cadres educate each other and do it in a revolutionary way.

The revolutionary concept of the cadres is erroneous because one supposes they are the intelligent ones, that they are generous people who will even die for the revolution and give it away to the masses. This is to me a very elitist conception, very authoritative. But I also acknowledge that from a dialectic position, in certain historic moments of the revolutionary struggle, the masses needed the "moment of the cadres."

Revolutionary Formation and Practice

G. Guevara-Niebla: I would like to point out that the problem of the "moment of the cadres" or the "military moments," which Paulo criticized, is not alienated from determined pedagogical results; they cannot be separated. Likewise the experience indicates to us that the one who uses a weapon in the struggle ends up becoming an authoritarian figure. This problem has not been solved, at least not in Latin America. One has to remember the "moments" of guerilla warfare that Mexico lived through and served to destroy in a certain sense the popular movements in the universities in the seventies.

P. Freire: I suggest that those who have not read the works by Amilcar Cabral on the struggle of Guinea Bissau take on the task of reviewing them. I am very much impressed with Amilcar's work like that of Che Guevara in the Bolivian news. Furthermore, they admired each other deeply. In Guinea Bissau the two met for the first time; they kept silence, they observed one another, and I would say it was a revolutionary love with clasped hands. (Even though Amilcar was short and Guevara was an extraordinary specimen of a man). They shared a love based on the revolution. And most interesting of all, they were similar in many other respect—both were eminent pedagogues, great educators of the revolution. For example, Amilcar never retreated from his task of politics and discussion when he arrived at the front in the struggle in Guinea Bissau. In his grove he evaluated the struggle, listening to shots and arguing with guerrillas, not only about military questions but about other things as well. There did not exist a military plan in Guinea Bissau in which Amilcar was not involved. He always evaluated the struggle, and he also discussed cultural, general educational, and political problems and took advantage of every moment to create a global vision.

On one occasion I had a long interview with six young men who had worked with Amilcar when they were sixteen or seventeen years old and I asked one of them, "What impressed you most about Amilcar?" He gave me an answer that I am going to share with you and that's kind of cute. The young man commented, "Look comrade Paulo Freire, what impressed me most about comrade Cabral was the following: my reality was located about six hundred meters from where I was whereas Amilcar's reality was always six years ahead of him." The young man gave me an example which I will repeat: "One day I was with the fellows on the battle front and comrade Cabral arrived and called all of us together to have a chat. Everyone went 'under cover.' [This gentlemen is very African; 'under' for these men is where the Africans converse sitting under the sun.] And comrade Cabral suddenly said, I need to take two hundred of you away from the battle front to Guinea Conakry." This is where the institute was located. One of the boys replied that it was strange to take two hundred men from the front lines. Cabral explained that it was inevitable that they be trained like a new species, different than battle but fundamentally like it. The boy commented, "What battle could be more important than this one?" and Cabral answered, "You have to study in Conakry, take a course there and then return." The boy gave Cabral every typical

Latin American reason for not going: "But comrade Cabral, first we have to expel the colonialists and then we can educate ourselves. In other words, fight first and only after we have victory can we think of educating ourselves. And this way," the boy continued, "we will not lose the war." Cabral expressed emphatically that in order not to lose the war, they had to go to Conakry (there he gave the fundamental explanation). He said, "Look, this struggle will not be won by my generation or by yours. But it will be won by the generation that is now five or six years old. This generation will win the struggle with a few of us still alive, and for the new generation to win the struggle, it will need scientific knowledge that your generation does not have, since the logistics of the struggle have entailed the use of war material that needs a certain level of scientific knowledge that your generation does not have. These new instruments of war require a basic knowledge of mathematical calculations which you do not have. Second, after winning the struggle, we must have a minimal number of people prepared, because the oppressor never trained us intellectually." For this reason during the struggle, Amilcar sent five hundred boys simultaneously to Cuba, the Soviet Union, and East Germany. These boys attended primary school in Cuba or learned how to pilot planes or studied mathematics. It was exactly this that marked Cabral with a prophetic vision. (Here prophetic has nothing to do with any transcendental dimension, but means instead the capacity to foresee the future based on a good knowledge of the present. The prophet or the prophetess is a person who can see your future so consciously that he or she can look into tomorrow). Cabral had an extraordinary vision of the pedagogical dimension of struggle. Because of this there has never existed for me a separation between the elements of struggle of liberation as a political act, as a cultural fact, and as a cultural factor. (This would provoke a semester of discussion in an academic seminar. The cultural expression of the struggles could be discussed as one part and as another, an analysis could be made of the cultural expression of transformation and its role as a factor of cultural change.)

University Hemophilia and Curricular Desires

G. Villaseñor: At the risk of perhaps repeating what has already been said about the curriculum since I was not here at the beginning, I remember something Gilberto Guevara said only a few days ago which seemed to me to be very important. We are looking for something to be done so that higher education will become an element of transformation. The curricula certainly are created with the idea of a contamination-free university, of a chaste university, but the problem is generally who creates the curricula. We, the teachers, do. Guevara pointed out a fundamental problem: until a few years ago, the university fed from its professors, from its own graduates, and we are now facing the phenomenon of professors who have not had any contact with the reality beyond the university. This allows them to read the reality first in order to be able to read the curricula later. What happens is that endogamy and academic incest one generated and the same university family interbreed its own children until they become hemophilic. This creates a problem for the university. Its internal reputation is established without any vital contact from outside the university. And on the other hand, we find a concrete case that exists in our country—the National Program for Higher Education, which made a detailed analysis of the demand for professionals in industry, commerce, banks, etc., in order that courses of study and programs could be modified accordingly. What I want to say is that when we are presented with a program for the universities that is not made for university students, as is the case to which I am referring, I know that such a program results from a real survey. We may not agree with its objectives, but it is a real survey of what reality is for these student. By bringing this reality into the university, the university is converted not into a means of transformation but one of confirmation of the system with which we, the university community, do not agree. We do not agree in part because of the ideological and visceral problems which we consider to be bad—the ones that are reinforcing the system and what we must connect with; but on the other hand, the same social structure does not allow us to connect with that reality. If we want to survive, we have to work in the university; we cannot be working in the pharmaceutical industry at the same time. The same system leads us to become enclosed. We will have to deal with this problem and also the problem of what an adequate relation would be between the education of professionals and socioeconomic reality. At present, if we wanted practical solutions, we wouldn't have any, not even efficiently predesigned. This problem occurred to me when I began to listen to discussion about curricula that is based on reading texts, not contexts; the endogamy in the university makes us prepare professionals who will continue to read texts, but the moment they leave the university they rapidly learn how to read contexts.

A. Fernández: In reality, your presentation touches on the problem of empty terminology on which the curricula is fundamentally based. In fact, I mentioned before that it was difficult to separate Paulo Freire's thought and practice from the two fronts, which were also pointed out by Gilberto—the symbolic structure and the forces that search for power.

Freirian Epistemology and Curricular Technicism

A. Fernández: Paulo's case is an illustration of the matter that we are discussing since his, concepts of a liberatory education, and pedagogy of the oppressed and consciousness (among others) delineate a continuous dialectical process of struggle in two different fields: one entailing the reconstruction of language, and the other involving ideology expressed in precise terminology that undoubtedly will be depleted and refilled with meanings in an ongoing process of participation by diverse oppressed groups. This leads us to one of the cardinal points in Paulo's way of thinking, which would like to mention before he gives his opinion on this subject. Paulo Freire forms his epistemology in a practical manner based on an idea—force. His epistemology is located in the practice of education in search of a liberation, a phrase that is also filled and emptied of content through the vicissitudes of social interplay. Paulo has been pursued and constantly asked about his method with the intent, not often malicious, of classifying or cataloging him under the headings of adult education or literacy studies and actually excluding him from other educational domains, such as the university. Nevertheless, the epistemology that underlies all the practice and thought of Paulo in some way points to a complete pedagogy,—several aspects of which will help in the development of this discussion on Curriculum and Society.

Let us begin by commenting that in Mexico we have seen how groups advance in their tasks and in their search for domains within the curriculum that they have formed, sometimes choosing the axis of the curriculum that is really represented inadequately. These groups consider the curriculum as a point of arrival, not of departure. And even though they have managed to provide liberating possibilities or allowed criticism of the liberating pedagogy, they actually fulfilled their curricular task once the new curriculum was formalized; in other words, it became a plan and study program. Its implementation over the past fifteen years or so has widely demonstrated that the inertia of the formalized curriculum has distorted and sometimes depleted the meaning of the emancipating intention.

It is in discussions of the curriculum that Paulo has given a great contribution. With the intention of putting the curriculum up for discussion and relating it to the university sphere, I would like to and systematically, summarize carefully some of the epistemological pillars of the work of Paulo Freire. I will try to show the Freirian conception of education as an act of knowledge.

For Paulo Freire, reality may seem a subjective, automatic, socially disarrayed illusion, since it is the reality of the oppressor—here the terms of his first period of practice are respoken—it is the reality of domination; of a domination that one learns day-by-day. Paulo opposes and proposes in this sense the reelaboration of that oppressive reality, which in the end will simplify the comprehension of the world. Liberating education is obtained only by subverting the oppressing reality, in other words, by filling the concepts of pedagogy with new liberating forces.

Paulo is a political pedagogue and a pedagogical politician in that he firmly believes. He believes in truth and objectivity, but he maintains that truth and objectivity can only concentrate on a struggle for freedom, a struggle for emancipation from the dominant power. Consequently, the knowledge that Paulo encourages is through transformation and the subversion of knowledge itself. Knowledge is "deposited" in textbooks, as has already been mentioned; it is separated from contextual reality. From this Freire concludes that the concept and practice of "banking" education is the dominating praxis. He warns that this practice does form or inform but rather domesticates those to whom the knowledge is directed. On the other hand, Paulo Freire has preached and practiced that reality and knowledge should be essentially *problematized*—a term that has also been emptied of all critical content and is now used for anything, even to speak of arithmetic problems. Nevertheless, for Paulo Freire, to problematize is the waiting room of the transformation, not of the solution to the problem ("problem solving"). Reality and knowledge have been problematized by the students and the teachers, in order for their apprehension to correspond to prevailing interests. Paulo Freire argues that a critical comprehension of the world should induce—but not in a deterministic form—the conformation of an anarchist educational organization and a political participation for the transformation of the world itself.

Lastly, for Paulo—to give an exaggerated summary—the forms through which knowledge is apprehended in reality determine and ease the political ideological position; although this is not visible at times, it can be found in either of the two forms I mentioned and discussed yesterday—the form of social and educational reproduction or renewal.

The ideas presented above have barely touched on some of the foundations of Paulo Freire's epistemology; they help us understand curricular reality and its practice which has been the focus of many expectations of Mexican education since the movements in 1968.

P. Freire: It is a pleasure when one feels that he is well interpreted. I remember once in Stockholm, Sweden, I attended a seminar where a Swede did analysis of Paulo Freire. (There was a simultaneous interpreting service into English which was very fast; it was carried out by a Swedish woman who seemed to be more of a translating machine than a human being. In the end I commented on this with her and she got mad at me.) I continued to concentrate as much as possible on what "seemed" to be, accoding to the translation, rather than what was meant to be. I was anguished because I knew that in the end the person was going to ask me what I thought about it, and it was going to be difficult for me to answer since I had to remain courteous to a certain extent. Nevertheless, what I understood him to say seemed to be a misrepresentation of my work and I had to tell him so. I said, "Look here, what I heard during the past hour is an abstract of my thoughts and it seems to me that it is everything except me. It is a little bit of me but what ever little part of me is there is distorted to the point where I am not myself anymore." It was awful, but I had to say it. I do not understand how in a society, in a technologically highly advanced culture, it was possible for an intellectual to seal and deplete what you [Alfredo L. Fernández] enlarged and dynamically filled—the whole world of contradiction that is here inside, all that movement—like a good Latin American. He [Fernández] did the opposite. He based everything on pedagogical philosophies and managed to place his interpretation, above all, in little boxes.

Technical and Scientific Education in the University

Now, let us go back to your concern, which is also my concern, our concern: that is, we have had to overcome the incestuous situation described earlier. We must ask ourselves about a subject similar to the one Ortega y Gasset referred to in an idealistic fashion a long time ago, a subject that has not lost its meaning: the mission of the university. First of all, it seems to me that a universal mission does not exist in the university; this would lead to a metaphysical position within a class society. Here the university has a mission that would not exist in a revolutionary society. I always ask myself if the University of Albania is similar to Harvard and whether because of their differences it seems to me that one of them is wrong. Either way, as in Albania or Brazil, there are certain fundamental aspects of the university, and the manner in which they are to be addressed will be different. For example, I have the impression that the university has to worry about research and education. The art of knowledge must be organized as a function of these two moments of the gnosiological cycle—the coming to know the produced knowledge itself, and the creation of new knowledge. These two moments constitute education and cannot undergo dichotomy.

At this point, I believe we must worry about the professional, technical, and scientific training of young people. This training must be soaked, however, in a political comprehension of the technical and scientific training itself. The political clarity of the technical and scientific training or education at the university is necessary. It even seems to me, that from this point of view, the existence of any differences becomes deeply creative. The division between comprehension and perception is a requirement for the university. I think that it would be a very abnormal thing to have a homogeneous university, with all the university students thinking alike and having the same commitments. This would be a gross mistake, it would be appalling for our education, for the education of university students. This is why I found that one of the virtues—if you consider a virtue to be a quality that we ourselves have created and materialized—that has to be created and materialized within the university is tolerance. To part with the incestuous relationship we mentioned, we definitely need the virtue of tolerance, which is still scarce among us; we are almost always intolerant. For example, when someone thinks differently than we do, we state that that person is wrong. It is terrible to discover these things! It is evident for me that the difference within the university is deeply enriching, provided that this difference is lived with faith, loyalty, honesty, and integrity. We must not engage in controversy, however, we must dialogue. Instead of engaging in controversy about the difference, we must hold a dialogue about the difference. For it is very important that the young student perceives a different vision of reality and that this reality is not the same for all university students. In this manner, the young student will know that there is a diverse educational context within the university. Thus, his or her political and ideological education will be enssured. Probably, upon making my ideas known, some *revolutionarists*, not *revolutionaries*, are already sanctioning my bourgeois weakness. Nonetheless, I would claim that my "bourgeois weakness" is fundamentally a democratic and radical dimension of my personality.

On the other hand, we cannot separate technical training from political comprehension, because we cannot ignore what the purpose of this technical aspect is.

Ignorance of technology enriches the power of the "establishment." From the viewpoint of the dominant classes, the university could not anticipate itself. As Lenin said, to be a good political leader, one must be a good worker; I have never seen a good work leader who has not entered a factory or who does not comply with his or her work. To be good professional leaders and good university leaders, they must be the best academicians and the best professionals, not the worst.

The problem is really not whether we must train them to fulfill momentary demands efficiently, but rather that we must consider what is implied by anticipating what is going to be done. Not excluding what is being done now. It is not to deny momentary demands in terms of the future but to include these momentary demands in planning for the future. And here I do not believe that we must have market research—that is, we usually live in the country, the needs are very evident, we do not need polls, not even to go to the Ministry of Programming and Budget. We are able to perceive that many people suffer from so many problems and have so many needs.

We can take very general points of view which may prove correct. In this way we would link curriculum and professional practice with a far more politized activity of intellectual work, both within and outside the university.

I. Marbán: I think that we must resort to history to review what the educational process was like in Mexican universities in the sixties, relating it to the political process in the country during that period.

I believe that most of us were students and professors and took part in the elaboration of "quaint" programs with different characteristics and we were going change the world radically through these programs.

The first problem that we faced was the lack of professors for those programs, and not only that, but within a very short period, those programs became unfeasible in practical terms—that is, at a certain point we fell into an academic crisis in economics, sociology, and international relations. (We can also infer similar circumstances from the experience of the UAM [Metropolitan Autonomous University] or from other universities around the country.) The students we were training were not qualified for the job market. Simultaneous with what was happening in academia, the country was going through an extremely dynamic historical, ideological and political process. From 1968 [the year of great national unrest among students] to date, the Mexican social and political life changed drastically and with it, our vision of this life has been modified: we have moved from "good people and bad people" to a vastly complex life of social relations and processes. With this vision the concepts of state, power, *Charrismo* [a corrupt corporative unionism in Mexico], etc. The practice of knowledge and political practice lead to social reality and taint it with very many new elements: hegemonies, consensus, unions bureaucracy (where, for example, the *charros* [corrupt union leaders] were no longer *charros*, but union bureaucracy). Simultaneously, our educational programs were coming to a stalemate, and of course this also happened to the democratization of education.

What worries me most now is what is happening to us. At this moment there practically exists a consensus on the need to relate education to the job market, to plurality, etc. This is what I want to emphasize: Is that a very open challenge? Or have we assimilated this democratizating experience? Or rather, are we in the possibility of going further back from where we started?

F. Ortega: My speech will be in the opposite vein of Ignacio Marbán's. I would like to comment a bit on the possibility of having diversity of choice within discussions, as Emilio Ribes mentioned. I am also very glad to see that, after more than ten years, I have the opportunity to listen to a different Freire: a Freire to whom questions on higher education institutions are being posed, and not a Freire stating—as he did the first time he came to Mexico in Cuernavaca—"I don't know anything about these things." (At that time we were students and there were several hundreds of us, nuns and workers included, in the area of "moral awareness.") Now I am very pleased that at this moment a series of reflections about another Freire experience emerges. It is precisely on this that I would like to ponder—in part to question, in part to reflect. My comments refer to what we could call Freire's pedagogical theory, if Paulo Freire would allow it to be so called. This theory referred to reflections that emerged from experiences not within the educational institution of the university but within a broader educational environment. Paulo offered a series of concepts that we all know and that had a great impact at the beginning of the '70s and are still very much in force.

I believe that the result of the meetings with Paulo Freire was abandoned by the groups themselves who were working for some time in blue-collar neighborhoods, in part because of the limitations of the social processes in all of the countries. There was a need to resort to other means, other techniques, to achieve a more or less certain liberating effect. (At that time our commitment was expressed as "a revolutionary dream.")

When many of us entered colleges or universities, we felt that we didn't have the right approach to the concrete problems of everyday professional experience. The terminology seemed alienating. For example, the term *curriculum* is not ours; it is an American term and nobody knows what it means. We generally use it to refer to our old term of *study plans* and *programs* [planes y programas de estudio]. As far as I am concerned, this term had to be questioned and analyzed. Nonetheless, for the purposes of this discussion, I would use it to mean "the institutional life."

From this perspective, the theory resulting from Freire's experiences is not only limited to the university, but it also dissolves the moment professors want to establish a dialogue or a dialectic relationship with the students. At this point one of the most fallacious questions emerged, which leads me to the following question: What does Paulo Freire do the moment he is in a university institution (struggling now within a concrete university), where there is a guiding, negotiating management system—a system that because of its characteristics and historical nature (as Gilberto Guevara pointed out, although he did not develop the subject), ends up limiting democratic work and also, very often, research and education? Furthermore, the moment when a professor pretends to link educational practice to a series of problems that could, at a given moment, help the subject really to understand the context (real life and classroom), the restrictions come in. Then, repeating my question to Paulo, I would ask, What is your experience now? What are your reflections on this experience within the university environment?

A. Fernández: Would somebody like to comment on Ignacio Marbán's statement in order to enrich the social analysis of the context, with different interpretations of experiences, or perhaps in any other way?

Freedom of Teaching and Formation

P. Freire: Pluralism is not an easy project. It is difficult to set up pluralistic work teams. It is evident that pluralism within the university entails positions that are not only different but also antagonistic. In the university there may be professors who are highly reactionary or radical. The matter, in my judgment, is the discussion of their own positions with the students; the student have all the right to have a reactionary professor. (I don't know if you have heard about a conversation that Mao Tse-tung had with one of his nieces. The subject of the conversation was as follows: the niece told her uncle that she was very mad because there were reactionaries in her school and she had read reactionary comments on one of the blackboards. Mao Tse-tung asked her, "How many students are in your school?" She answered that there were 5,000. He then said, "Well, now I know what made you mad." She replied, "We left the classroom for a few minutes and when we came back it said on the blackboard, 'Long live Chiang Kai-Shek!' I got mad and I thought that it was absurd for someone to write that." Mao Tse-tong asked her, "How many reactionaries among the 5,000 students do you think are in the school?" And she answered, "At least 3." And the uncle asked, "And you, 4997 students, what are you doing against those three? Well, let me tell you: it seems to me that you are trying to deny them the right to speak and therefore you furtively 'Long live Chiang Kai-Shek!' wrote on the blackboard. You should prove that your values are better and not criticize or condemn those of your opponents." The niece did not understand and said to Mao Tse-tung, "Uncle, every day I grow more disappointed with you."

The university environment should be pluralistic and dialogical, even though sometimes polemics, controversy, and quarrels live together. Formation is a problem of curriculum and also of the understanding of what is curriculum. Many teachers think that curriculum is just a set of subjects, methods, and techniques, when it really embodies a comprehensive philosophical, political, and epistemological understanding of the pedagogical task. It is clear that the struggle for a curriculum implies pressure on the dominating classes and the educator state. Pressure must be applied to widen the areas necessary for our struggle. Sometimes we professors, men and women, fight a lot and organize ourselves to fight over salary improvement, which is absolutely basic; there are also strikes. (Currently in Brazil all professors from the public universities are on strike, demanding higher salaries. Inflation is more than 220 percent per year.) It seems, however, that the struggle has to go beyond the economic aspect and towards cultural and political dimensions. I think that we should go on strike to demand better research conditions, to improve working conditions, to reorient the technical and scientific ability of the students, and to preserve cultural identity.

Virtual, Real and Hidden Curricula

A. Fernández: The previous issues are part of the daily lives of teachers and students. In the effort to explore curricular activities that use the educational environment, we could take advantage of the witticism of Paulo Freire in introducing issues and problems where advancement could be made in the formulation of options. I assume that any educational level is important for the subject we are dealing with. Pedagogical distortion provoked by the mass media (such as television on basic education) as well as demands by the government and private industry for the technicalization of intermediate and higher education represent similar moments in the struggle over curricular development. The subject does not end, however; it is rich in topics and problems. Next I will mention some of them and I'll ask you to share this task. We will start with the following: the existing educational concept of a curricular exploration or implementation and the one that is really practiced. Also the problem of participation—not only the participation that is structured in a bureaucratic, academic, and administrative manner, but also the real one that surpasses these spheres and that is often the determining factor in the curricular effort and results. Moreover, the participating groups with different ideas about society, about education, elect to impose one of these ideas in curricular practice over other ideas. There is also the matter of the assimilation of knowledge, of its organization, of its conception, of its structuring, and of its relationship with the students. Neither should we ignore the conservative and transforming functions, even with a radical flag, of curricular development.

How the curriculum actually structures learning is extremely important, and this is not reduced just to what normally has been understood as the systematization of teaching and learning, but is also the specific happening of learning itself. It would be important to investigate where "radical" knowledge packages, as a source of learning, could lead, as Paulo Freire would say, toward a banking form of education.

It is of particular importance to highlight the social and cultural orientation of education—a subject that has been widely discussed, and it is in the same curricular practice that these concepts are implicitly shaped. One will always read a social and cultural notion within the curricular reality and this will not necessarily correspond to the intentions of its authors and actors.

The problem of values in Mexican society (as another subject) came dramatically to the fore during the successive devaluations in 1982. The Secretariat of Public Education had been very sensible to this phenomenon years before and had promoted research over cultural values and curriculum. It was known that the values of the nation—however they may have been understood—were rapidly wearing out. Some negative findings were discovered, but nothing was heard about applying corrective measures. In fact, the problem of values is one of the challenges faced in curricular development and the effect on students of the various curricular manifestations is not yet known. The hidden form of the curriculum has been denounced but its functioning is unknown.

It is of vital importance to consider the real and predictable role of teachers and students, because curricular reality is build upon the relationship between teachers and students. I think that this has been discussed too little and, sometimes, it has been ignored altogether, because it is considered to be solely a political matter alien to curricular reality itself, although it seems to me that it is one of its components.

The social-historical contexts of the curriculum and the areas we could discuss build and drive curricular development as an emancipating project. In fact, there is a strong tension between curriculum and needs, because the latter are perceived differently, as being popular, national, radical, cultural, ideal, etc. In some way, the prevailing conceptions assume that if a relationship to needs is not established, the curriculum is not accomplishing its purpose. According to the attitude mentioned by Guillermo Villaseñor that these needs are in the core of the state apparatus itself, it is assumed that curricular reality could be fulfilling those needs without any intercession or mediation. Actually, one of the richest polemics involved in understanding the curriculum is the rationalization of the interplay between present and absent actors in curricular reality.

There are other topics in the phenomenology of curriculum and society that we could discuss widely; however, I think that those already mentioned present a great wealth and vast complexity that serve to open up the discussion.

Democratization of Higher Education

F. Rueda: I have one comment and a question for Professor Freire. For some time the possibility of the democratization of education in Mexico has been discussed. The accumulated experiences have been diverse. For instance, at the present moment we have the experience, which we are going through and read about daily in the newspapers, of the Autonomous University of Guerrero. This experience of the democratization of education in institutional terms was intended to be a global educational project. (The debate over democratization essentially started in Mexico in 1968. It acquired strength during the '70s). Now then, my question has to do with curriculum, but it also has to do with the possibility in a dominating system such as ours of democratizing an institution and defining it socially. (I will go deeper into this question.)

Yesterday, I thought I understood, with the help of Gilberto Guevara, that the educational institution acquires a new function; it acquires a new reality that is far from being an institution that reproduces the dominating ideology to one that accepts a group of social forces that participates (there) and that takes advantage of the areas they open. I thought I understood from José Angel Pescador, however, that this was not true, but that it appeared to be a kind refunctionalization of the university or an institutionalization of university criticism. It seems they called it 'corestriction—corestriction' of the theory, of social forces, or of many things. Actually, the problem of 'corestriction' is a basic discussion for us, because from it arises the possibility of formulating certain educational projects such as that of higher education.

Reproductive University

Once again the specific question I would pose refers to the verification that the university fulfills—in global terms, a reproductive function of ideology, culture, of many more things. When we compare this idea with reality, however, it does not always comes out like this. We also notice that not only in Mexico or in Latin America, but all over the world, a "very special" relationship exists between the type of university graduate and his ability to enter the job market, or between having a labor qualification and the functioning of the job market, or between the existing social structure and the inarticulate demand of the professional groups, or between the evaluation of the academic degree and its school or labor overpromotion.

Now then, the question to which we with Paulo's help and that of the participants can perhaps find a solution is about the idea that all of us who want to think, formulate or improve a different educational project have related to the previous type of problems. I am aware and cannot deny that it is necessary to educate people *well*, even though they will work in a capitalist system; but it will be necessary to educate them *critically* in order for them to think about what they will do professionally. This does not exhaust the problems of an educational project, however, because it also has to do with the curriculum way beyond the design (on paper) of its contents. Obviously, there is an enormous social environment that is present and is part of this reality. What should we do?

Lastly, I have another worry: Are we thinking about the need of a political struggle, not only pedagogical in terms of pedagogical practice but also in terms of political struggle itself? The educational project, we know, is a political struggle in the sense that social forces in one sense or another, act on, move, and lead certain educational policies. Also I must mention that in the management of the university itself there are coexisting efforts that take different directions. Thus, all this conditions, shapes, and intervenes in an educational project.

P. Freire: Look, now I want to listen to the Mexican opinions before giving mine. Fernando Jiménez gave me a book that deals with the role of authoritarianism within the UNAM. Also José Angel Pescador has something to say about technical training and the politics of its formation. Moreover, I assume that Felipe, you, all of you could say much. I want to listen to you a little more, because I am interested in knowing how you interpret these matters.

Co-option and Reply Area

E. Ribes: There are two issues that I would like to comment on and that are related to some problems dealt with yesterday and to another one problem directly related to the curriculum. One of them is the issue of co-option within the educational institution and how we can take advantage of the pedagogical-political area that the institution itself opens up for their contradictions. In the case of our university, at least in my experience, a very peculiar phenomenon appears—the discrepancy between the discourse that wishes to neutralize co-option and its daily practice. I think that this one of the central points—the political dimension of academic activity. Generally, the Mexican left, whenever dealing with the problem of the democratization of the university, has taken the problem from the top and not from the bottom—that is they have focused on the problem of the democratization of government structures and not on the daily practice of all those who are part of the institution. This has resulted many times in sterile confrontations because obviously, the probability that some day the University Board by self-decree will democratize itself is extremely low, I believe. However, this is a permanent and continuous goal of the progressive groups within the university. This discrepancy, besides being very serious, produces a bouncing phenomenon of self–co-option: people remain neutralized because they automatically assume an administrative inertia that is absorbed in the process it is trying to erase. Thus, we see that the professor who demands the democratization of teaching is the professor who most of the time is worst prepared academ-ically. A false dichotomy is created and a confrontation is set up between academic ability and democratic ability. This assimilation into management as an operational inertia results in the professor turning into a systematic reproducer of educational practices that supposedly he should fight and resist. This is the professor who has a text, a doctrine; who is not tolerant; who criticizes without knowing whom he or she is criticizing. Obviously this situation suggests first step in university reform, would be to start from the bottom. That is, in the same manner that you mentioned yesterday the possibility of joining the 'gay' movement or the ecologists' movement, we could also join the movement of the academics inside, because academicians are already considered as "the 'gays' within the university."

I believe that one of the things that political parties should do would be to attract academics (which they have not yet done), not only by improving salaries but also by improving general working conditions and daily practice, the practice of politics within the university. This also implies in some manner a change in the nature of the teaching process; that is, I think that the democratization of practice in front of the student does not mean asking the students what they want us to teach them. If they can tell us that, then there is no reason for them to be in the university. There is an obvious difference in level, simply because some of us got there before other—it is a problem of time and not of any other kind. But it is a problem to work out the dilemma jointly in order to start learning and modifying the process of knowledge—its transmission as well as its production. That implies something that seems paradoxical: that is to change the ideological practices of the students, because our revolutionary students are most deeply reactionary when they are examined as participants of a really deep change in education practice. These are the students who, on the day you decide not to have exams or to eliminate the banking class of a professor to which you can come just to listen and you ask them to learn through doing, discussing, analyzing—on that day these students automatically turn against you. I think that is a very important dimension.

Reconsideration of Formation and Treaching

I want to go back to something that you mentioned concerning Amīlcar Cabral and the problem of anticipation: The relationship of university to society and of the curriculum to needs. I think that this relationship is always analyzed in a very linear manner; it is considered to be a fixed correspondence in what is actually a continually changing process. The only way to solve this apparent problem is to look at the six years instead of looking at the six hundred meters—that is, to get ahead, to anticipate and this means training the graduates from our universities in order for them to be able to enter and survive in society.

It Does Not Cost to Dream. Education Does

E. Aragón: To continue with the image used yesterday, it would be worthwhile to ask what happened to our dreams. I think that to start with, we should answer that we do not assimilate our democratizating experiences. Maybe we have not understood many things, in spite of having lived through them. We have been actors to some degree, but that does not allow us to pretend that we have entirely understood these situations. We have already posed several problems, but we have many more. We have not grasped the nature of democracy in an institution of higher education.

Regarding democratization, there is a lot still to be analyzed and thus to be done, in order to reach a conclusion. There is no assimilation of our experiences; probably some of us have not had adequate means to judge our results. There are some situations showing the results, and a lot of prudishness and complicity—and mean shared complicities—can be found in our actions and attitudes. When something goes wrong, we say, like those who are in charge of overcoming Mexico's crisis, we are truly recovering. Never has anyone mentioned that we were losing something, and even when we feel something goes wrong, we say that we are recovering, without clarifying what the evil is that we are recovering from, and mainly where we are going to. We have lacked, again, this perspicacy, which, besides, would be greatly important for other reasons. For example, to be able to locate ourselves not in a retrospective analysis but in a prospective one is an area where I feel we are not strong enough. We don't know where to go, simply because we don't know how to evaluate how we have advanced.

We need to guide this apparent direction of the discussion, the question about where higher education is going. There are many aspects of and questions related to this subject, but we should begin with an answer to Ignacio Marbán's question: let's assimilate our experience. To begin with, let's see if this has been a truly democrating experience. The term *democrating* is somewhat self-gratifying, but we are sure that in some cases these experiences have been extremely authoritarian and have entailed a number of problems that we have left out and that I want to clarify. I think this is the problem!

Toward an Integral Interpretation?

J. Pescador O.: I think it is convenient now to try to answer the questions that have been raised and to postpone the reflections on Freire's statements on the problem of authoritarianism and democracy. Accordingly, let's see what has been happening in the university for the last fifteen years. We may note that there have been very significant qualitative changes.

My interpretation of the Mexican university views it as an entire institution and not as an isolated entity within a subsystem. In that sense, it seems to me that the contradictions generated gave some favorable responses to the trend toward democratization. Both in popular universities (those called "democratic universities") and in the Universidad Nacional Autónoma de México [National Autonomous University of Mexico (UNAM)], Autónoma Metropolitana [Metropolitan Autonomous University (UAM)], and the Instituo Politécnico Nacional [National Polytechnic Institute (IPN)], very significant changes have taken place and I would like to mention them.

1.   One of the most important changes is that the idea of curriculum has developed not as a plan or as a program, but as a conception of the university. In 1975, more than ten years ago, *Foro Universitario* [the monthly journal of the left-wing workers' union, STUNAM, at the UNAM] was discussing the problem of what is understood by *curriculum*, and how it has to be interpreted within the universities.

2.   The relationships between workers and authorities are not yet perfect since pressures like strikes are still used to demand improved labor conditions. The presence of a university union is an undeniable force, however, which with some limitations—and probably mistakes—is a very positive force. I say this because we must not mistakenly link university unionism with strict academic quality, but rather with the working and operating conditions of the university and as a reflection of what is happening in our society.

3. I would give a different interpretation to the statement that professionals are not finding many positions in the job market because of their training. We are getting used to this alleged truth when we know that deep inside, unemployment among the educated is also related to the market. Nevertheless, we accept the official line without criticism and the permanent argument of conditioning the university according to the economic project and not to a particular university project linked to the essential needs of the majority.

4. We have advanced greatly in the democratization processes. Apart from a definition of democracy because this would lead to a very serious problem, it seems that a conformist culture exists among faculty members in this country, and it has gradually changed as a result of the faculty's participation in union struggles, demanding improved labor conditions and claiming the need to transform the university. The truth is that this conformist attitude has been abandoned or at least has decreased, and by and large, this seems to be very significant progress. Speaking about the panorama of higher education, for example, when Mexican banks became part of the state, a forum[1] was organized to offer alternative points of view linking efficiency and a purpose of justice to the tasks of higher education and to an economic fact as concrete as the nationalized banks. The answers were not as elaborate as they could have been, but at least this forum generated some concern that apparently precipitated some action in the government sector.

5. Another very important question is how to move from a scheme of mere representation to one

involving major participation. We cannot say we have totally achieved this, but in collegial bodies of the universities there is the possibility of this participation turning into effective representation. What has happened is that it is normally criticized as an authoritarian collegial structure where there is only representation and no participation, but I consider that within the union organizations themselves, there has been pressure with the purpose of evoking important changes. It seems that this pressure can be found both at higher and lower levels in all universities. And this pressure must be understood in the context of the greater social changes that the country is experiencing in a very radical way as a result of the current crisis. There are efforts to tailor the university project according to the model of country where the great capital is going to define the productive structure; financial resources will continue to be used (through state banking) for the projects yielding greater income from a cost-benefit point of view. From this perspective, it is logical to demand a more "efficient" university. And it seems to me that the university, although it has not assimilated all of these democratization efforts, has at least established very important bases to be able to refuse such a project. We can illustrate this by considering the project of university reform currentlyunderway in the UNAM.[2] Those who know the project have questioned it; however, the fact of questioning it does not mean that we reject it entirely. Even though this has been a willing effort of planning, even though this has been a directed exercise, some groups in the community have had the opportunity to start working within this project.

These are some of the important domains to be taken advantage of. We must assimilate some of the changes of the past years in order to systematize them and reflect on them so that we can build a vision for the future. What we cannot afford to do is to isolate ourselves, as some have done regarding the project of reform in UNAM's case, because this project is the instrument that is going to define a concrete conception of the university of tomorrow. For that reason, the responsibility of the university community of this institution has increased. It is not just a matter of taking part in the project but of knowing that to some extent a trial or experiment of creating a new model for a national university is being carried out. This is why these efforts—union participation, representation, curriculum discussion, expansion of programs, and teacher training—must be strengthened. we must take advantage of the domains still open for us and of the fact that the university has to seize this possibility of analyzing at this moment its contradictions in order to generate more democratic alternatives.

Criticism of Educational Criticism

E. Margolis: Well, sometimes I am really surprised to see the optimism with which many people refer to the problem of university reform, because I have attended many meetings with interesting people, with people who have argued socially, who are leading these types of meetings and what one can see at the end is a lack of love to be able to do this. Then we realize that this is a resolution from the top where very well dressed persons, with a very good "social history" are needed. We, the intellectuals, are asked to give ideas on the goodness and feasibility of alternative university systems. And from there, everybody starts to work like mad on the curriculum—its components, its social reality, its theory and practice—but as a matter of fact, at least as far as I am concerned in my experience in the university, in every university with reforms of this type there exists a complicity that ensures the lack of real participation of students and teachers. We cannot find work programs and most of the time external reality is devouring everything that has been left inside. This means that where a lack of teachers might exist, there is now a complicity between teacher and pupil. This complicity involves a real teacher giving a lesson but no student willing or having the time to study or the money for buying books, or able to part from his or her family, or free of personal problems to be able to go to class and attend as we did before. When curriculum comes into style, however, everybody seizes this topic, leaving aside the need to go further ahead and to understand what is going on. Thus, I would ask Paulo Freire how he sees reality and how at a certain moment he could use this difficulty in understanding reality to address these kinds of problems.

A. Camarena: My comment is very simple. While my colleague was talking, I had an idea. He said that we were in the university as an outside reality; I think that unfortunately this is not so. We cannot forget that we have an ideological position. It is also true that, suddenly in the university there exists a schism between the discourse about what our educational projects pretend to be and our own power position in the institution. Even more, we should ask, going back to what Professor Freire mentioned regarding the curriculum, what concept and educational projects are we proposing, what kind of struggle will we enter into, and what power do we have?

I think we have spent a long time and have irresponsibly wasted our educational projects, whether these were revolutionary or not.

G. Guevara-Niebla: Yesterday I was expressing my gratitude to Paulo Freire because he has opened for us a perspective on many conceptions in the socialist domain that revolutionary groups had closed for us. The possibility of thinking that we could have a type of revolutionary education, that we could carry out a revolutionary militancy through education, opens up for us a new perspective. It seems to me that this is an opportunity, a revelation of a new domain, of a new optimistic horizon for those of us working in education.

I pointed out that we still have some conceptions from the past—very strong conceptions that view school and education as fatally chained to reproductive tasks. Examples of these are the old understanding of the ideological apparatus of the state and the old economicism, which stated that all types of education were entirely determined by the economic structure. These conceptions tied us up. Freire comes and reveals a new horizon for us, this new perspective of political intervention in education. I only want to mention that, going back slightly to what Ignacio Marbán was presenting, how can we recover the past in a meeting of this sort, since those of us who ten years ago were proposing a possible flight from the classrooms or from research sites have been the target of harsh criticisms from our own colleagues, and have suffered severe intolerances, and for years we have lived in the midst of great intolerance here in the university, and this, friends, can be kept in silence. The truth, however, is that we live in a noncritical environment, where there is no debate, no self-criticism, as Elīas Margolis mentioned. There is no political debate, then Paulo Freire comes and opens up for us the possibility of discussing our vital problems. On the contrary, when socialists forces meet and debate, there is an underlying and nonmoralizing policy. I am sorry, but when social forces meet, self-censorship and mechanisms of fear prevail! In the university itself we perceive an atmosphere of intolerance. Besides, I would like to bring up something that we must bear in mind: unlike what happened in the '60s—and I am not trying to establish the time when we were students as the best— there is no political debate in the university, no political information, and very often the university is more passive than any other public entity, and here no doubt we are searching. Paulo is understanding and this is what is new in Paulo's thoughts.

Paulo comes first to the university and then poses the question of how to generate a liberating pedagogy within formal education, within college institutions. I consider that this analysis has existed in our country for fifteen years, but in a very disorganized manner, a nonorganic manner, because political parties didn't assume the struggle in culture as their problem, because trenches were never dug in the university for waging a cultural struggle. Trenches were dug for other purposes but nobody discussed the university's essential activity.

The level of our conceptual development about the university has been very poor. The university has changed, and what we did was to recover a very old speech on university reform, which was the banner of the reactionary liberal Catholics during the '30s and '40s. This discourse is the rebuke for a democratizing govern-ment. That's o.k., but that liberal program was never thoroughly analyzed, because, my friends, that was not a socialist program. That liberal program seems to have prevailed in the university. Emilio Ribes is right in mentioning a fundamental problem: our militant socialists end up discussing the university's administrative problems and are permanently trapped inside a circle or in some self-consuming activity, thus not allowing us to see the ultimate perspective that could clarify how the university (as a cultural institution) is contributing to cultural and social change. Thus, in what way are we trying to modify the social movement of the university?

I think that the discussion of this matter, which is the focal point of the university, has been very poor. I believe that the university has changed and I said it three days ago in a discussion we had in the Iztapalapa unit of the UAM. There I debated that we have to take into account the phenomenon of university bureaucratization. Nowadays there are new social players in the university— the bureaucrats—who didn't exist in 1968. They didn't exist as they do today. I do not want to use this term to classify, but simply to say that there is an enormously thick layer of officials. As far as professors are concerned, for example, no one realizes that in '68—slightly before— there were only sixty-five full-time professors in the university (yes, in this university). The concept of professor changed entirely; the old professor does not exist any more, that professor who came to teach at the university has been removed. The new player is the full-time professor—full-time according to terms of the position or according to the hours spent in the university—and he or she is devoted to teaching as his or her job. Maybe this is a new fact, which on a practical level modifies the entire nature of the university. Furthermore, the students have also changed.

If we refer to statistics, we can analyze them and we cannot say that something has changed: students who still are sons of employees, professionals, small merchants, etc., account for 70 percent of those enrolled. But two things are ignored when analyzing the new condition of the student. The first is that radical changes have occurred in the urban layers: the lower middle class has violently lowered its standard of living during the last fifteen years; new layers have emerged but with a clearly lower standard of living. Secondly, professional tasks have become proletarian and thus the student condition has also become "proletarian" (I warn you that we must be careful when we use this term), although statistically students seem to be still part of families of the same social group.

All this creates the right conditions for a more radical program within the university, one that can surpass liberalism, and this is what the left wing (generally all leftist forces) is not aware of. I do not mean that a more radical program is possible just because of the material conditions of the new players at the university, mainly students and faculty, but it is possible to take into account the new general conditions of intellectual work.

Now, our statement should extend to encompass the two prevailing ideologies: liberalism and anarchism. The reactionary Catholic liberalism has taken up anarchist positions. In the leftist groups we can often find anarchists disguised as socialists. People criticizing all types of institutionality, all kinds of normativity, all kinds of hierarchy, all kinds of order. Well, I would ask myself whether, if the left is really fighting to eliminate all legal, hierarchical, institutional, orderly form, this is not socialism but anarchism; there are persons who accept this. Many socialists hold these anarchist ideas, however, and fight within socialist groups.

Furthermore, another prevailing conceptual position is corporatism. Unionism is a practice generated by the university's growth. To dissent is politically legitimate, moral and valid. We fight for unionism, we create unions, but we do not need to make a noncritical defense of unionism. In Mexico, unionism has adopted corporatist manners that must be criticized without adopting antiunionist postures, and we need to talk explicitly about what corporativism means, because we never mention it. We defend the past without criticism. But we are linked to the past, we are umbilically linked to the past, and this is, as far as I am concerned, what keeps us tied down.

These thoughts I have expresssed freely for all my colleagues. It seems to me that what we effectively need are the right conditions for an honest and comprehensive discussion, not excluding or disqualifying anyone on moral grounds.

All rejection of the fight is reactionary; we need an optimistic program, we need to create conditions for tolerance, for open discussions without fear.

R. Glazman: I would like to refer to José Angel Pescador's position regarding universities, which I find tinged with excessive optimism. José Angel points out that in recent times a university space for discussion has opened up.

First I would like to characterize the university in terms of three periods—before 1968, from 1968 to 1976, and 1976 to 1983. Probably then we may speak easily with optimism. Specifically, no room for doubt has been opened up, but also no room for action. In a certain way it seems to me that this discussion will be carried out within the limits of what Marcuse or Eggleston would designate as "repressive tolerance": there are professors and researchers who are allowed to speak up because their statements are "useful," because it is necessary for the system to have some opponents, who are not allowed to act in terms of making proposals and carrying out actions of academic policy. On the other hand, José Angel Pescador thinks that the curriculum has been permeated with the idea of a university project. I would venture to say that the definition of such university projects is not stated. Lastly, Pescador mentioned that there no longer exists a conformist culture among university professors, but the truth is that there is a dreadful fear of one. The university professor is afraid to talk because the structure of the university administration has created such a situation that every time researchers or professors express themselves, they fear eventual reprisals. There are officials who have manifested their opposition to critical academics.

All this has created a situation in which professors have no real representation. At this moment when several university members present knowledge as a tool of power, as the only tool of power that university members have, there is a reaction from the bureaucratic sectors, which also recognize the power of knowledge and fill the academic space with their administrative positions.

The Absent University

F. Jiménez Mier y Terán: Well, I will refer fundamentally to the UNAM, an institution that I would characterize as the "Absent University"—that is, a university that in the crucial moments of the country— 1968 as the exception that confirms the rule—has been absent from change. Thus when independence was being conceived, by immediate orders of the Major Faculty, the precursor to the current University Council, a publication was issued stating that Miguel Hidalgo y Costilla never studied in the university classrooms. This was done to avoid the charge that the university had been in any way involved in the independence movement in opposition to religion, to the country, and to the king.

During the Mexican Revolution, the university once more stayed out, and this is very clearly explained by Gilberto Guevara in one of his books. Later, the Mexican university got its autonomy because it opposed in a reactionary manner the revolutionary measures of the governments of that time. Later on, in the '30s, the university was one of the main enemies of Cardenas, who was trying to implement the project of a socialist education. This opposition was made to protect the university's autonomy and the principle of freedom of professorship.

In the '40s, when the government entirely changed the university totally supported it, and from that date on the university kept in step with the state plans, with the exception of 1968 and a few other moments.

Another reflection I would like to express, related to the previous one, is that it is frequently thought that the university is an abstract entity, and thus, the university would have to carry out the revolution, to say something. However, this is not so. The university is not an abstract entity. It is a very complex institution, integrating many sectors, I would even say that it includes many gangs. A lot is said about the university community, but, I think that this sociological category does not explain anything at all. Instead, it confuses a lot because when we speak about a community, it is implied that all university members share the same interests, which obviously is not true. When talking about a university community, we automatically pretend to eliminate the ideological, philosophical, and political struggle that exists within the institution, a real struggle that prevents the configuration of a community.

Going on to the curriculum, I'd like to refer to the courses of study, and to begin, I'd like to express this: I think that Paulo Freire's "banking *educational* conception" prevails in the UNAM. I say this is so in the best of cases, since at this time I would be content if only the teacher deposited knowledge in the student, and the student gathered and assimilated this knowledge. We cannot even reach that point, however. In practice a sort of understanding has been established in which the teacher, who supposedly is the one who has the knowledge and must teach, simply does not do it. On the other hand, the student, who supposedly is the one who has to learn, does not. We must add that the teacher who has not taught is shameless when it comes to demanding the approval of a course. This is entirely understandable in the context of the UNAM which has gradually been establishing the optimal conditions to foster this harmful understanding.

All this is closely linked to most of the curricula in force in the UNAM, which tend more and more toward the division of knowledge, toward divorcing theory from practice, toward strengthening the conservative character of the university. I will briefly refer to three elements obstructing the modification of the curricula: First, the university bureaucracy, which I have already mentioned (including technical councils and the University Council) and which I consider to be bigger and stronger every day. Second, the power of the faculty, which is none other than than the power of ignorance, the power of the professor repeating word after word, year after year, the same lesson, preventing all discussion, all debate. Finally, the apathy and disbelief of the students who feel more and more pushed aside. If students have to learn, it is said, what can they contribute to implement changes in the curricula? All this is within the framework of a university governed according to an obsolete authoritarian university law per se—the same law that finds its origin in a speech, with very interesting ideological content, made by the then dean of the university, Alfonso Caso. He stated that the university must be a technical institution separated from politics and thus its authorities must be technical, not political. In establishing such a sophism, he concluded that a technical university having technical functions must be governed by the best technicians. These supposedly technical authorities are the University Council, the technical councils of departments and schools, and later also research technical councils. Now, these councils supposedly have technically exclusive tasks; one of them is the approval of the curricula. If, as a matter of fact, these curricula were approved on the basis of technical criteria, the reality in our university would be very different. Since this is not the case, what definitely takes part in the elaboration of the curricula are precisely these political criteria, the political struggles that occur mainly within the technical councils and that in the end open up spaces for the several political groups in order to study such and such an author or such and such a subject. It is in this way that incongruous curricula having important flaws and undetected duplicities in bibliography, for example, are made. Once a professor told me that in the School of Political and Social Sciences the *Eighteenth Brumaire* by Bonaparte is read eighteen times. What is serious about this is that the political character of the technical councils is not accepted, in spite of the fact that their political tasks must undoubtedly be supported by technical tasks that allow the correct implementation of the decisions made. Learning these techniques, however—I am referring concretely to the techniques for the development of the curricula—requires interest and work and constant study. And this is currently of no interest to the UNAM. On the contrary, technical work is improvised and often despised; even though there is someone prepared to do it, this person is left aside or even taken from his or her job. I end my reflections by saying that I consider that in such a complex university as the UNAM it might still be possible for the development and approval of curricula in accordance with reality. This is one of the reasons why we must consider that within the UNAM, in spite of its conservative character, social domains still wait to be conquered, to be worked in the Freirian sense of the word.

Specificity of the Freirian Epistemology

A. Fernández: I think that the comments of this meeting leaned toward the fundamental concept of Paulo's work and thought, toward the management and use of educational domains as domains for political mobilization and for the search for power. Before giving the word to Paulo, I would like to ask the audience if someone would like to remark on or enrichen this circle of presentations.

M. Escobar: Well, I think that we can see a fundamental epistemological problem here. I recall the definition that Paulo gives of himself, as "a pilgrim of the obvious," in so far as he takes what is obvious and shows that the obviousness is not such. There is something very important in this, which can be found in the Freirian practice, and when we try to probe into it, I believe we make many mistakes. For me the most important fact from Paulo is that he dialectically knew and has known how to take part in reality and step away from it to analyze it, finding pertinent theoretical elements, and going back to it in order to transform it, implying a transformation of reality itself. It is important to talk about a transformation of oneself, because sometimes we speak of something as being collective, and in this collective body we can supposedly and implicitly find what is individual, but that is not true. This sense of the individual being implicit within a collective body is lacking. The obviousness, on an epistemological level, is presented in relation to what is understood as the object of knowledge. The fundamental problem is found in the fact that most professors—facing not an objective reality, but an analysis of objective reality found in books and articles turn this search into the object of knowledge, and in a struggle for power simply turn it into a struggle over the representations that we have of reality. Then the dialogue, which should emerge from such analysis, is no longer a mediated dialogue leading to reality; it is an aligning, metaphysical "dialogue" about an abstract "reality" that has no meaning.

There are many mistakes made of this kind. We forget that the obvious thing is not so obvious and thus I believe that in the fundamental mistakes we often make is our attempt to repeat the ideas of Freire, Gramsci, and Amílcar Cabral. This simply turns us into authoritarian and dogmatic repeaters, dogmatizing reality, dogmatizing ourselves, and simply becoming agents apart from reality. In all this we can see the problem of authority. And if we add the constant denial of affection, because I believe that deep down the problem of authority is also a psycho-analytic problem, this is the cause of our mismanagement of reality. So as a result this mismanagement of authority allows us to accept easily what Alfredo Fernández mentioned in relation to Televisa [the major private mass media consortium], (which I call "Yanquivisa," to be more exact). From there we could state that we must ask ourselves what we listen to, and what we read, not what we think, because in fact we are not thinking, we are simply repeating what we hear. Thus the problem between curriculum and society has to do with the relationship between knowledge and power, the trans-mittal of knowledge and the creation of knowledge, etc.

Fernando Jiménez mentioned that professors are not even banking actors, and I think this is true, because there exists a dichotomy between education as a political action and as a knowledge action inserted into a historical reality, and this dichotomy in turn allows the political struggle to be alienated from academics.

In short, I think that we lack a true commitment. It is very easy to tell the students to organize themselves, but we as professors are more and more outside the political struggle and not even part of the academic struggle. I feel that the best weapon to fight technocracy is to commit ourselves to an academic project. It is logical for the central power not to be interested in discussing academic aspects since authoritarian decisions are very easily made.

Thus, this discussion about the curriculum deeply affects our lives. We must reconsider our dialectical selves, the way in which we are reading our reality, transforming it, and attempting to wade through it. In Latin America, I believe that it is important to know to what extent we are allowing ourselves to be challenged by a reality that poses fundamental problems and a reality that invites us and demands an answer from us. The theoretical instrument is very important since we cannot deny the progress of science and technology.

Freire's Recapitulation

A. Fernández: I wonder if anyone would like to comment on this or any other matter. If not, Paulo could continue with the discussion and formulate a conclusion. Miguel spoke about some crucial points relating to the epistemology of the Freirian action. I would ask Paulo to recapitulate the topics considered, especially on the concept of the educational domain. The problem of domains also refers to the measuring of the progress and the setbacks of the Mexican university. The concept of domain in relation to the curriculum offers many nonexploited possibilities where we could still make many advances in progressive pedagogy or in radical pedagogy. Domain is currently reduced to the staticness of the curricular fact, however, and the renewal lines do not attempt to reconquer conservative curricular realities. Thus this morning's discussion enrichens our dreams and expectations for change and transformation. It is because of this that I would like to ask Paulo for a conclusion, namely the critique of domesticating pedagogy.

P. Freire: First of all, I think that the second part of the morning held geat value for you as Mexicans. And do not doubt that certain things mentioned here are related to Brazil, and with stituations that are occurring there. It is a shame—since our American cousins have unspeakable interests on this respect—that we are still living in

Latin America without knowing each other. The time has come to accelerate an exchange of knowledge.

The question concerning the use of the institutional domain is very important. One could create a whole theory about this; however the need exists to emphasize that all the use of spaces is critically political and ideologically biased. Therefore, it is not possible to attempt to use a domain and ignore the critical conception made by someone else about the same domain. This is daily life and we must not be simplistic. For example, liberals are struggling for space and try to fill it and their criticism is an implicit criticism of the use of space, but it is a criticism that does not go beyond the space itself. Consequently, institutional domain (in our case, the university's domain) liberally occupied won't go beyond the limit or limits of the educational subsystem.

One criticism of the use of the space by someone intending something more than a liberal position will go beyond the domain, surpassing the spaces of the institutional domain, reach the context of the social system. In other words, a liberal criticism of institutional space in a bourgeois society is equivalent to the reforms within the domain itself. (I acknowledge that sometimes the only possibility is to assume the liberal criticism of the handling of spaces. And this is so, because to do politics implies to live critically the historical, political, ideological, and social limitations demanded and posed by politics itself. What is fundamental is to take advantage of the situation and try to create, not in a self-willing manner, a new historical climate to transcend liberal criticism.)

The other criticism of the institutional domain comes from the idea that the institutional domain serves in part as a pretext and as a means of reaching a deep radical criticism of the capitalist system. I find myself in this position. Radical use of the domain must imply from the beginning exploiting the operational margin within the limits of the domain aiming at reaching the greatest criticism. This has to do with a greater comprehension of the curriculum. It has to do with the possibilities we may have within the university to exercise a criticism that cannot remain on a purely verbal level. The criticism of the university institutional domain cannot stay on a purely verbal level per se; on the contrary what we have to do, ensuring the coherence that you (Alfredo Fernández) identified as lacking, is to find a moment in which the relation between discourse and practice reaches an optimal level. In other words, when the verb is also the praxis. If we are now so far from coherence between speech and action, then there is nothing left but to obtain a relationship between practice and the verbal expression of the practice.

I was asked, for example, what to do with university professors. I myself was a university professor for a long time, long before the coup in Brazil. But the professor I have become is not the professor I was. It couldn't be! I would be horrible! Even exile had a fantastic role in my reeducation. It taught me that radicalization was a fundamental course and enabled me to go through different experiences as a university professor in different parts of the world, in Latin America, in the United States, in Canada, in Europe, in Africa, and in Asia. I had teaching experiences in all of these parts of the world and they provided me with an immense store of educational information. For example, I experienced many of the things you mentioned here with the students at that time, in different domains.

As for the general acceptance of the curriculum, I remember when young people rebelled all around the world in 1968 without intentionally coordinating their actions. In 1968, students in Mexico were not telephoning young people at Harvard, or in Colombia, in Prague, in Brazil; nevertheless, they carried out more or less the same movement, it was impressive. I also remember that communication between world universities was non-existent and it was unbelievably easy for dominant classes to repress world movements. For example, in Europe a whole dialogic pedagogy was even developed having nothing to do with me, and it simply meant that dialogue started after the programmatic and curricular content had been set. On the contrary, I propose that the dialogue begins at the very moment when I am asked about the curriculum. Then, what was the action of the authorities of the prevailing classes? They partially fulfilled the demands of young people. I will illustrate it with a metaphor. Prevailing calsses got on the bus at the beginning of the trip, and young people got on the bus in the middle of it. The first part of the trip was acknowledged and premeditated for those holding power and the young accepted a trip that was already established. A liberal dialogue will always accept established rules, but a radical dialogue (which must be rejected) will never hold rules critically. In the first case, it is the authority with power who will decide what the dialogue will be about. For us a dialogue has to be the subject of a dialogue.

To fill a domain is not merely a political action. I must clarify certain things. Emilio Ribes said something that is very important for me and has to do with the defense of rigorousness. Emilio was talking about how it is necessary for young students to come to the university and find professors with enough scientific competence to provide students with meaningful learning. He added that if this was so, there wouldn't be any need to justify the existence of a professor. Now, I also believe that a professor loses his or her role when he or she leaves the role of teaching and its content up to the students. However, I am convinced of something: in a course students should have much to show from their experience in social practice. And this has a lot to do with the scientific task. If professors are not able to find in the students' practice and experience something that has to do with our scientific discipline we will not be qualified to hold two or three days of dialogue with the students about experiences outside the university and from that create some programmatic content that would extend the curriculum needed for their studies. In fact, if we are not able to do this—that is, if we are not able to talk about their common experience, turning it into philosophy— then we do not know what to do with our science.

For me this is the way to "start a dialogue on the content of a dialogue" and not to start the dialogue about the content we are proposing. The second proposition includes a liberal position. The revolutionary position has to go even further: "It must get on the bus at the starting point and not during the run." Let's analyze a paradox: getting on the bus four stops later, would satisfy both liberals and authoritarian revolutionaries. There are many examples about the total conviction held by some revolutionaries of their authoritarianism.[3]

We can find thousands of people among us making Marxist speeches but nevertheless defending an authoritarian position. Thus I would like to state that, for different reasons, the liberals are very pleased when debating with an authoritarian revolutionary, because in the end they are talking the same language and they know the conclusion beforehand. In contrast, open dialogue has no end. There are conversers, however, who previously establish the dialogue and the person who refuses to accept it falls into misconception and foolishnes.

Dialogue is my teaching tool, I use it at different levels of college and postgraduate studies. I have used it in different universities: in Brazil, in Switzerland, in Canada, in the United States, etc. Miguel Escobar could confirm this since he has taken part in some of them.

To finish, all I have to say is that this morning was as rich as or even more so than yesterday's. I consider that there were many opportunities for you to express several things that have to be said and must continue being said. I would conclude by suggesting something: to try to hold dialogue meetings with actors, even if they are totally different. I am aware that I have been used as a political excuse to gather several different groups in a discussion. I have no doubt that I am an excuse for a group of people who meet, discuss, and never overcome their difficulties. I have had the experience of being an excuse. I always remember a meeting I attended one weekend in Frankfurt with three rival leftist groups. They attended because I was going to serve as mediator. It was great! I learned many things, and probably after that weekend they continued to be rivals, but maybe they also started to understand each other.

3

The Role of the Intellectuals

The Role of the Intellectuals in the University

M. Escobar: In this part we will center on the debate about the role that intellectuals play within the university. When we organized this seminar about education and society we thought that today's subject would allow us to synthesize and delve deeply into the statements made during the two previous days. Because when we question ourselves about the function that we—professors, administrators, and students—develop in the university, inevitably we will have to discuss important and controversial items such as the political function of intellectuals in the university domain, the relationship between the academic project and politics, the political definition of the academics, the power expressions in the university sanctuary or haven, and the essence of the university which today gives us shelter, that is, ideological pluralism.

The analysis of the dialectical link between the intellectual function and power is one of the pillars of Gramscian thought. For Gramsci, there is a minimum of intellectual creative activity in all physical work, even in the most humble and mechanical type or work. Thus all men and women are intellectuals, but not all of them function in a society as intellectuals. The specialized categories in the intellectual function come out of the relationship with social classes and, due to their nature, may possess certain autonomy of the intellectuals from the class that begets them.

From these Gramscian statements, which influence Paulo Freire's thinking to a large extent, we can extract some points, such as the political dimension which, implicitly or explicitly, is carried out by intellectual practice; and the historical-political determination of intellectual practice, which, when developed in a concrete society cannot be marginally analyzed from the society in which it is born and to which it dialectically belongs.

In this sense it is essential for our debate to take into account the specificity of the university context, which although immersed in a concrete society nonetheless retains a relative autonomy from it. Many times this is expressed in complex contradictions.

Among these contradictions, we could point to the dichotomy between theory and practice in the university domain and the presumed lack of political definition of the academics (supposedly because of the "neutrality" of scientific knowledge) which contradicts the practice of their power function in the classroom, etc. The Freirian praxis has been radical in denouncing these false positions; it has especially emphasized the political role played by educators in any formative process.

Freire's insistence on this point has provoked some authors—like Vanilda Paiva [a Brazilian scholar], for example—to try to destroy Freire's pedagogy, reducing it to a reformist questioning of the student-teacher relationship, leaving aside important aspects such as the forms of political expression.

The above illustrates one of the typical contradictions of university domains in Latin America. In practice academics have the title of intellectuals but they do not exercise the function. Like Vanilda Paiva, many Latin American intellectuals are not familiar with the historical development of the Freirian praxis. They have not even read all of his books, remaining only with *Education #sas the Practice of Freedom,* but not reading *Extension or Communication? Pedagogy of the Oppressed, Cultural Action for Liberation and Other Writings, Letters to Guinea-Bissau* and *The Importance of Reading and the Liberation Process.*[1] As Paulo Freire said, we intellectuals do not even read one book per year—that is, read it well. If we did that, it would be dangerous for the status quo.

Well, I believe that these general statements can lay the foundations for our discussion today.

E. Margolis: I would be very interested in makinq a statement that seems elementary, although on some occasions it has lent itself to certain misunderstandings. Our role as intellectuals, with the assumption that we would respond minimally to this premise, would be to ask ourselves what is the particular type, what should the necessary politics be in institutions of higher education. According to my judgment, it would be a special type of politics. This is the central idea that I wish to propose to you: the politics that we should make are academic politics. The course, the contents, the role of institutions of higher education have to be defined starting from the great title of academic politics. Frequently, we have confused this task of making politics with the problem of "step aside, here I come"—that is, the battle, in every case well intended, even well designed and well proposed, over the changes in the forms of government. If we would examine those positions after some years of consistently pursuing these objectives, we would find that the democratizing projects have basically consisted of administrative changes, but not of changes in academic politics. That is, they stop making politics with capital letters to make it with small letters. With this the change is simply established, it can be located in the change of persons and not in the method, which, according to my opinion, should prevail.

To summarize, there is no democracy in institutions of higher education unless it is accompanied by the academic project. Furthermore, a trade union or social organization that does not have an academic conception and does not act within the university environment the way it is and is confused with a purely business entity turns into one more part of university bureaucracy, into one more gear. It then does not have anything that is substantially different from what the university bureaucracy represents, but it is expressed in the regulation, in the articulation, of a concrete part of the university—the labor relationship

Politics and Academic Policies

P. Freire: I would like to ask you some questions to try to clarify my understanding or perception of your speech: what specifically is an academic policy? And what is the relationship between politics and academic policy? Because if you talk about academic policy it is because it seems to you that there is another policy that is not academic; otherwise it would not need to be called "academic." But when it is specifically called "academic," it is suggested that there is another one that is not "academic." Then for you, what would be the relationship between academic policy and the policy given in connection with society and power structures, within which, as subsystems, academic policy is found?

E. Margolis: What I understand as academic policy, or to make an academic policy, is to have a project that necessarily starts from a definition of what the university is or what higher education is. It would include the different tasks that today we accept as university tasks and naturally their social insertion. This would lead us to a wider universe, that is, to what society is and should be and to what we frequently call social needs. To summarize academic policy includes the course followed by the institution, the tasks that specifically must be performed in research, in teaching, in the spreading of culture, and in university extension. This role of the university should be recognized because the political struggle has frequently been reduced to a transformation, to a more or less acute incident because of the moment's needs. Even because of problems of self-defense, the ways of government have been transferred to a first level, without these modifications really having any reper-cussions on the strictly academic environment. It is said that the role of the university is being questioned—that is, on essential matters—but there are avant-garde movements that are even trying to play the role of a political party. They assume, misrepresenting their function, the role of a class, of a political party.

The problem would basically rest in having a sufficiently clear analysis in order to be able to say, as far as specificity allows us to, what the university should specifically do: that would be an academic policy. And naturally, what would be the difference, what is the relationship between this policy, between what is possible and what is desirable, in the relationship between university and society, between university and state? This is something that is always disputed, with small or large rapprochements. At the present moment we have in

Mexico one of the most paradoxical situations that we can find. With a more or less autonomous tradition firmly established, we find today that autonomy is questioned— not in its formal aspect, because it was even promoted on a constitutional level. It is being questioned on the measure that the financing of higher education tasks is conditioned. That is, anything they wish to do can be done about this task, as long as it is what the Secretariat of Public Education wishes to do.

P. Freire: When I asked you that question, I was not trying to ignore a certain specificity of political matters in the academic environment. The basis of my question lies, first of all, in the impossibility that an academic policy that mocks history, the social aspect, the general political aspects, should exist. Thus, according to my judgment, a university that is beyond and above the social and political system of the society where it exists is unfeasible, and if this is not possible, it means that every academic policy basically has a point of reference and that is the global system.

To be more explicit, I would say to you that for me it is absolutely unfeasible that the University of Havana would be in Brazilia and of course it is abolutely unfeasible that the University of Brazilia would be in Havana. With this I want to say that an autonomous academic policy is unthinkable. Now, in the second place, there are academic policies that, according to my judgment, reflect political and ideological positions, within the academy's own understanding. For example, you could have an academic policy that although very serious would also be deeply scientific. What do I mean by this? I am referring to a mystifying and mystical understanding of science and starting from it, you could have a whole academic schedule, but you could also have a position or an academic policy of a basist nature,[2] with an academic policy that should propose the leadership of academic work constantly thrown into the popular strata of the society where the mentioned academy is, in such a way that the policy would be oriented precisely in the sense of that naive criticism made to me—a criticism that is not aware of my position and introduces me as if I were a "basist," as if I thought that the popular classes and only they own the truth. I have never said that.

Academic Policy and Global Political Context

Now then, in contrast, you could have (and this is very common) a deeply elitist academic policy—an academy that orients its work toward teaching and research, based on an elitist concern. Necessarily, this policy would be concurrent with a major policy, also originating in the society with elitist power—a policy that would amount to closing the academy's doors to the sons and daughters of farmers and workers and would almost be an insolent policy from the dominating class, but it would also be a policy, a policy no doubt. You could also have an academic policy that was neither populist nor elitist and that disguised itself as a little of both, which would be a greater ambiguity than the populist ambiguity; it would be a policy without a definition. By this I mean that I believe that an academic policy has "N" possibilities.

With these hypotheses that I presented, a little caricaturized, I want to make clear that from my point of view, there is no exclusive policy from the academy. There is no metaphysical essence of the academy that allows us to say: this is the quality that defines academic policy anywhere, in any history, in any domain, any time.

That is, there is no historicity in the academy, to the extent that the academy itself cannot be seen outside the global political context to which it belongs.

Respect for Political Pluralism in the University

To me, in this sense, it is very important to be aware of political pluralism in the academy, thereby avoiding our segregation in political terms, for example, from intellectuals with whom we do not share our project. I am not saying that we should hide our political position in the academy. For example, I belong to a political party in Brazil and the students know this; there is no reason to hide it. What I cannot do is change the academic policy of the university where I work for the policy of the Workers' Party and I must respect the students who do not have anything to do with that party. In fact, they refuse even to think about the Workers' Party.

This is interesting: I cannot dissociate my militancy from my pedagogic practice, of course I can't. In the university process, however, I cannot take advantage of the space that the university provides to proselytize for the party I belong to. For example, for this reason, the academic policy has a specificity that other areas do not have. I even believe that the more pluralistic we are in this sense the better it will be. This does not mean that the academic policy should be a "quilt"—no, not at all. I believe that academic policy has to assert a certain political option to extend to the academy, but basically, it seems to me that in academic policy there must be a respect for positions that are not necessarily like the ones formally defined in academic policy. That is why I asked you that question.

E. Margolis: I totally agree with what you have said.

Politicity of University Autonomy

G. Villaseñor: The course that this discussion is taking may be very important, because I believe that the essence of the work of those persons who would like to make politics through the academy lies here. With regard to what Eliezer mentioned, I very much agree with his basic idea, because we have found a problem, the handling of which has been passed on to me, especially in the use of a concept of autonomy that is managed according to specific historical interests. I remember a phrase first used in 1976 regarding autonomy, which soon became famous: "Academic matters are not negotiable." Behind this pressure were the problems that led to the rather long strike that ended with the police entering C.U. [University City, the main campus of the UNAM] in 1977. Actually, what was being challenged was the idea that the university is autonomous. This idea is not only something that is managed by those who, in a given moment, use the university as a political element to serve the class in power, but also it is something that we as members of the university carry very deeply rooted at a subconscious or unconscious level, since it gratifies our egos for us to feel as members of the university, because we feel there is a privileged environment inside, where knowledge is created and we seek to feel it.

Academic Policy and Historical
Conditions of Social Structure

Regarding the question that Paulo Freire asked Eliezer about what he understands university policy or academic policy to be, I believe that we could try to define what academic policy is. But we cannot do this if we do not place our starting point outside the university, trying to analyze historical conditions and giving to the word *historicity* all the wealth it has.

The historical conditions of social structure must be known and within that structure, we should know what are the historical conditions of the subordinated classes, the domesticated classes. Starting from the discovery of the historical situation of the subordinated classes and the relationship that this has to its social needs, we can start to propose what an academic policy would be with a markedly *instrumental*, not *instrumentalist* character, which would turn the university into one of the instruments of the majority classes.

I know that this proposal is very difficult to accept since the university would turn into an instrument of the class struggle. From this perspective, what happens to the essence of the university? What happens to the essence of knowledge? And what happens to the essence of the creation of knowledge? There are many problems involved here that, under certain circumstances or in certain environments, create roadblocks. How is it possible to conceive of the university as one of these instruments, not generically speaking of the majority classes but of one class? Nevertheless, I think that this is the only way we can understand the creation of an academic policy. This way, the task of the formation of professionals will be in keeping with the historical position of the majority classes. The developing of research and the spreading of culture will be other basic functions of the university.

I believe that this would certainly provide the conceptual foundations and policies for the drafting of an academic policy. I believe, however, that the work of whoever is interested in making the university into a transformative element cannot be exhausted in developing an academic policy such as the one described. There is another series of policies, which we could call "university policies" in general. For instance, it is necessary to develop a systematic policy for the course of the universities. It is not possible to develop an academic policy to serve the majority classes when we have a university bureaucracy that does not allow the development of an academic policy such as the one that has been proposed. And in practice, we are constantly suffering rebuffs because the authorities or the groups of university bureaucrats do not allow the development of these types of programs, etc. It is seen then that something (academic policy) cannot be done outside of what a global university policy would be. We can not draft an academic policy without a university policy.

The development of an academic policy entails bearing in mind the need, mentioned before, of joining the different and the antagonist. Among the problems presented here is the one mentioned by Eliezer: "Step aside, here I come." Many times too much importance is given to the person who is "different" from me, occupying the position I could fill, thus clearly favoring the antagonist. What happens then is that relatively democratic people, turn into our main enemy and thus our university struggle is exhausted in malicious gossip among democratic people with leftist criteria. Thus, we do not have time to draft a serious academic policy because it may be more important to knock down the person from this fraction of the party, not to let the person from the other fraction be promoted, etc., and with that our possibilities are worn out.

I think that at least partially this is due to the following: of how many of us who work in the university can it be said that we would have "university vocation"?

That is, how many think that what happens in the university is something vital, something important in their life? There are many people, and this is taken as a fact, for whom the university is an element of promotion and social prestige. To others, to be in the university is a factor in their political promotion, a step in their political career, whether it is from the left or the right. But in these cases, if this or that happens to the university, those persons are not significantly affected, because the university is not something vital for them; it is not something that is a significant part of their lives, there is no university vocation. And if to all this we add the fact that the ones who are different are not capable of joining together against the antagonist, then we do create chaos, because with all those problems the academic policy does not have any possibilities of coming through.

I wanted to present this long proposal because these are concerns that I have been accumulating as a result of what has been said; I believe that in some manner we have a way out through what Eliezer has said. I consider all this important from the perspective of the relationship between university work and politics.

The Experience of Risk, Essence of Creativity

P. Freire: There are certain impasses that I do not know how to overcome. Undoubtedly, to me the expression of academic policy implies the problem of power. The question of power is in the center of reflection, of practice, of academic policy. It is about a skillful internal power that does not exist by itself, since internal power or the struggle of internal conflicts in the haven of the academy is conditioned by the major external powers, by the ideological or political powers, etc., by the dreams that feed the search for power. I think that in order for a certain academic policy to be fruitful, however, it would be basic that this policy implied a vital physical and organic experience for those who participate. An experience of risk—that is, of an academy that does not sacrifice itself because it does not take the risk of creating. Not much can be expected, because there is no creativity without the risk of creating. Creation is not something that simply appears. I would say that creation does not occur, it does not happen—it is a risk that must be taken in order to create. I would even assert that is is impossible to live without risks. Therefore for me creativity is a basic condition of existence. Existence is more than simply living; that is why creation is risky. But there is no risk when the possibility of overcoming fear does not exist, that is, how is it possible to take a risk if one does not have the conditions needed to face fear. You do not take the risk of facing fear if you do not have a minimal space of freedom; thus, without freedom, there is no academy. For instance, if you do not have the freedom to carry out your research and to asset that it is scientific, if you feel that there are absurd boundaries in front of you, that there are ideological platoons restraining you, then, what can you risk?

The matter of freedom is basic for the search, for the risk, and without this I think that an academic policy disappears. We cannot fall into a naive idealism, however, when thinking that it is possible to create a "province of freedom" outside a specific society where the material conditions of that society work against the affirmation of freedom. To the extent that the confirmation of freedom can, and almost always does, focus against the arbitrary power of the class who rules and imposes its ideology on the majority groups, the confirmation of freedom faces serious problems.

Thus, on one hand you feel that you have freedom in the university, but on the other, you see that freedom in the university does not exist by itself, because this would mean the acceptance of a whole and complete impossibility. This is an impasse: first I assert a need and later I discover that this need, which is freedom, is difficult to carry out and all this, according to my judgment, rotates around the question of power. Historically we have to taken into account, however, for "*n*" reasons, that the university domain is larger than the political domain. For instance, the domain is larger in secondary schools than in primary schools. We cannot compare with another university the domain of freedom that any of us have in this university community.

The Widening of Freedom Domains in the University

My question now would be the following: how to fight well internally, how to try to increase the internal struggle in the university overcoming that terrible problem of intolerance, how to overcome intolerance instead of decreasing the domain of a power who respects freedom more, on the contrary how to gain strength in order to create a different power from which it is possible also to create a different academic policy. If we do not win internal power in the university we will not be able to create this policy and that is obvious. Knowing that even though we will not be able to inaugurate an academic policy that contradicts global policy up front or even rid ourselves of the historical tradition according to which the academic domain is holier than any other educational subsystem, we could study the possibility of increasing, widening, or pushing the freedom domains to be debated in the academic ranks.

I believe that this is the basic aspect, since to the extent that I can testify before the students with whom I work, even this language which I am now using, for example, must be considered. The moment that I reject the possessive language which makes it possible to say *my* students, *my* programs, *my* seminars, *my* bibliography, and to the extent that I never talk about my students, about my program, about my seminar, about my bibliography, but that I always say "the students with whom I work" and to the extent that I try to see, if possible, in an ocean of freedom, to create and re-create. I say that, I try to have coherence between my speech and my practice and this attempt to have coherence as far as freedom of students is concerned, to respect my freedom, both in speech and in practice, is in itself a testimony to the need for a domain of freedom. Because of that, it is a pedagogic speech and the more we do this in very specific terms, while challenging ourselves as students and professors, with this policy we will be giving more of a real meaning, whatever the university policy may be, to the need for freedom, without idealisms and very concrete.

J. Pescador: There are some questions that Paulo Freire has stated that would deserve at least five more seminars. Therefore I consider it convenient to try to link a set of ideas that has been raised, to try to answer the concern about the role of intellectuals and, better said, of academic workers, since there is a not solely semantic difference between these designations.

These theses of domains, in spite of having been explored in advance, had not been proposed before as they have been during these three days, within the concept of revolutionary pedagogy. There are many questions that should be clarified and that appear to be contradictions, thus they deserve a dialectical analysis not based on formal logic. First, how is this revolutionary pedagogy compatible with an ideological plurality? Because ideological dissidance and tolerance are very different from the presence of different trends that can perhaps generate confusion concerning the search for a final objective, which in this case has been stated or proposed as the seizure of power.

The Specificity of the University Environment and the Power Struggles

The second question that I would like to propose is that it may be more convenient in the universities to search in this temporal and spatial location for a redistribution of initial power. From my point of view, this would facilitate the solution to many problems that have been proposed and to the existing antinomies between academy and policy, between labor union and university authorities, between teachers and students, as was mentioned yesterday. (What the student wants is one thing and what the teacher does is another.) The analysis of a political problem on university premises differs greatly from the analysis of a political problem outside the university. If for instance, the final objective is the seizure of power, then this proposes at least one modality of the class struggle that is totally different from the one given in the university environment.

The domains of militancy have also been mentioned here, but one of the clearer contradictions is that it is precisely the academic who tends to give up militancy. Yesterday it was mentioned that apparently during the last ten years the rupture of this conformism could already be seen. It is not only conformism, however, but also an absolute rejection of participation in certain political matters. If one is going to manage this type of problem, you start to discover all the domains in which you must act. The task is to make the academy at once more rigorous and less exclusive. We must work in this domain. Not to allow absenteeism or the nonfulfillment of professors' responsibilities—that is another domain where acting should be permanent. Another one would be not to allow this divorce between organizations of university workers and the students. But the problem is that when this ideological plurality is abstractly proposed, the doubt persists that precisely this conception opposes revolutionary pedagogy.

Dialogue is a basic concept that must be included in these reflections. Unfortunately, academic dialogue is very much conditioned to myths and taboos in the university.

It is possible that the basic educational level, in spite of being more under control and subject to a series of hierarchical and authoritarian mechanisms in decision making, has less myths. Guillermo Villaseñor pointed out three or four that still exist in all universities, without failing to recognize that significant positive changes have occurred during the past years. That's why he talked about the assimilation of democratization, expressed in expanded enrollment, increased resources, and the availability of full-time professors. Today, whom do university bureaucracies work for? If academic workers and intellectuals are entering the ranks of university bureaucracies, people who are more linked to the needs of professors within a different social project, they cannot necessarily work to serve a ruling class; thus they generate another contradiction within the university. This thesis of the seizure of power should be called the "redistribution of power," because power is above, but a way to redistribute it would be precisely to enter the directive organs.

When Paulo Freire was speaking about the experience of naïveté, the estimation of the risk and the measurement of freedom, he was recalling the experience of the University of Nayarit—a university that enjoyed freedom within its own environment, that assumed the risk and that changed the project, until finally, however, it was directly crushed by the more backward interests of that state. The estimation of risk was centered in the interior of the university and that was maybe a costly mistake, because the measurement of risk should not be a function of what is happening to the university, but of what is happening outside the institution.

When Eliezer Morales talked about the necessary changes in orientation, he was probably referring to the fact that these are made because of a project directly linked to the university, even though they carry an external intention. In a certain way a reinvention of power is necessary. Gilberto Guevara said it very clearly: university bureaucracies are a very old phenomenon, not a recent one. It is known that until a few years ago, university officers were in accord with the external political interests. Now the situation is starting to change, because of the pressure exerted on public institutions by private universities, whose alumni, day by day, are finding more positions in the ruling area of government.

Going back to contradictions, I will mention another one that seems basic and that sometimes provokes many reactions. I am referring to the harshness that must orient university actions. You don't live absolutist spontaneity, but sometimes work is done with very little urgency to analyze the consequences of a decision or of a series of acts and that has caused the university system as a whole, in spite of the advances recorded in certain areas, to simultaneously experience marked regressions such as authoritarianism, restrictions in the participation of curricular design, obsolescent teaching practices, the lack of contact between research and social projects, etc.

Ideological Tolerance as a Revolutionary Virtue

P. Freire: If you allow me, I would like to tell that for some time now I have been insisting in Brazil on this question of tolerances. Generally I would say, that according to my judgment, tolerance is a revolutionary virtue. This virtue is created. When you referred to a certain danger in ideological pluralism, I thought it would be appropriate to say what tolerance means to me. It is not a balancing act, to me it is something too important. I am convinced that intolerance, like a lack of virtue, has some basic places where it is generated, this is in a clear metaphorical language. One of these places is insecurity: emotional, psychological, political, ideological, and scientific insecurity. This assortment of insecurities tends to provoke me to assume a sectarian position, which means raising a defense wall around me, a wall with which I defend my truth, which I accept as the only truth, the one I have to impose upon others as deliverance for others. Since I am not so sure about my truth, however, I do not allow anyone to come close to my truth to ask about it, because just asking affects my truth, and this is because I am not sure of it.

The other place where intolerance is generated is in the lack of belief in other persons—that is, when I don't believe in the possibility others have of facing history.

Thus, for instance, I can not allow my students, and I say "my" on purpose, to be exposed to a bourgeois professor who analyzes bourgeois economy when I know that he will do so against Marxist analysis and thereby endanger the revolution I am defending. Now, what a damned revolution would that be if I cannot allow my students to be exposed to a dialogue with reactionary professors, even in a corridor or university hallway? And this because of the fear of taking the risk that all will become reactionaries. I don't think that this risk is possible.

There Is No Revolution Without Risks

Tolerance implies security in your position, security does not allow you to pretend to turn into a guardian of others, of freedom, and of the ethics of others. On the contrary, tolerance rests on the conviction that you have that without risks there is no revolution. What a hell dialectics would be if it tried to annul its adversary! It would be a dialectic that would paralyze history. What the authentic revolution is trying to do and has to do is to overcome the antagonistic contradictions through the radical transformation of the material structures of the society in which such contradictions are generated. But this is not about ending contradictions, because that would be like ending history, and there is no revolution that has such power.

For example, when we think of a society that has not fought or made its revolution, how would it be possible to accept this type of attitude that ends by inhibiting every process? This also happens in my country—not in my case because personally I am sixty-two years old and after all I said to myself that I have to be less frightened—but how many young people remain inhibited? This should not be, according to my judgment; it should not be. To me, it is something basic that students should know that there are epistemologies that differ from the epistemology defended by one. But why should I be the one who has to tell students about other epistemologies? Why shouldn't this be done by someone who defends his way of understanding the world, who can testify before the students about what he is and say that he has a different way of thinking from mine.

However, I would not like for someone here to think that I am defending a liberal position.

The Nicaraguan Revolution:
A Curious, Restless Revolution That Dreams

Risks are taken in the defense of plurality. There exists a risk in societies that have gone through a revolution that tolerance will be more like intolerance than tolerance. I don't want to tell you what I felt during my first visit to Nicaragua. Speaking in public I said, and I also said to myself, that the Nicaraguan revolution is a small baby girl, but it is not a girl only because she is two months old, but because she is very curious, because she is restless, because she asks questions, because she dreams, because she is not afraid of being questioned, because she wants to walk, because she wants to mature. Please do everything you can for this child to mature, but she should never grow old, never, because old age is the fear of being new and the fear of being new is the fear of freedom, it is the fear of a question, it is the fear of doubt.

Look my dear friends, one thing that I also learned in exile, maybe the best thing I learned, is that I could not continue being sure of my certainty. And what happened is that when I started not to be sure of my certainty, I started to be more sure, because the only way that you have of being sure is not being sure, and this is dialectical, it is not formal thought. I think that this is even what a revolution would have to do; the revolution should not be afraid of its adversary, it has to face him permanently.

I don't want anybody to tell me: Look, Paulo, you have never gone through an experience like this in your country, because there has never been a revolution in Brazil. But, for example, I was in Nicaragua last September and I repeated this when I spoke there and I said, look, I am very happy because I find that the Nicaraguan revolution is a young girl, still a young girl. A minister came to me and told me: Paulo, you were here four years ago, and now that you are back, tell me what positive things you have found. I answered with a testimony that seems basic to me: I talked to a young woman from the people on the street, she didn't know who I was and I asked her, "Do you like the revolution?" And without looking aside or turning her head (gestures that a Mexican would probably make before answering, gestures that students in the United States now make—I said what I am telling you now in public at the University of Massachusetts in February), the woman from Nicaragua simply looked at me and answered, "No, I don't like the revolution." I asked the students from Massachusetts: "How many of you would tell me that you don't like Professor Peter Parker if you were his students, how many? You would probably be afraid that he would fail you." Instead, this woman from the people was not afraid, and don't tell me that she said this because she was crazy. No, she was not crazy, she was experiencing a political atmosphere that granted her the right to be free.

I told the minister that I was answering his question with the answer the woman gave me, because to tell a foreigner that she didn't like the revolution was the best way to say that the revolution was good, because otherwise the woman would have been afraid to tell me that. Facts like these let me see reality better and not only through textbooks. For example, I am more interested in what the woman said than in a speech from the Minister of Education. The speech of this woman is better.

The Great Historical Subjects of the End of This Century

To conclude I would say that if they would leave— and I am afraid they will not do it—Nicaragua in peace, I would think that in many dimensions, Nicaragua would be like Cuba. The testimony given by Nicaragua must be understood; Nicaragua would not be what it is today if there wasn't Cuba. Cuba, for me, is an enormous and endless revolution and to me, the Nicaraguan revolution is giving much to the Cuban revolution, because before Nicaragua, Cuba, in the continent, only could look at itself. But now Cuba can look at other revolutions, which necessarily are different. This shows that a revolution is not imitated, it is made. A revolution is not metaphysical, it is historical. I think that if Nicaragua would be left alone, this would be a great revolution, one of the main subjects of the end of the century. Because I am not afraid to say that there are some central historical subjects at this end of the century that are proposed more on the left than on the right—such as the subject of power, the subject of the reinvention of power and of the plain seizure of power, the subject of subjectivity, what is its role. Subjectivity is a very old historical subject, it is a subject that goes hand-in-hand with the history of human thinking until today, a subject to which Marx gave a definitive position, a definitive speech that is sometimes distorted when Marx's position is put not in a dialectical dimension for the understanding of subjectivity toward objectivity, but as if it were mechanical. This is a subject that is linked to the problem of freedom, a basic problem that is proposed politically in socialist experiences. I don't believe in the incompatibility between socialism and freedom; there is compatibility between one thing and the other.

University Intellectuals, Prisoners of the Cartesian Discourse

E. Ribes: I would like to take up again the point of academic policy and how we could draft it within the domains offered by the university. I think that generally in our daily lives, but also in our political and professional lives, we are prisoners of the Cartesian discourse: we always detach the idea of action. I think that maybe to face the problem of this new university class, I would not say that the academics are the ones who turned into administrators, but that the administrators are attending or visiting our academy. There are some administrators placed there to pretend, but the danger is not that the academics are in administration, but that there are no administrators in the academy; a discussion has to be carried out with accountants and business administrators, with people who only know how to compare columns of figures, of empty numbers that do not say anything, only if they agree or not with a certain entry from a certain group. I think that the problem does not imply that a redistribution strategy is excluded from power, as José Angel Pescador mentioned. That is, not to decline to agree with certain intermediate levels of directorship within the institution will always allow the opening of new domains or to take advantage of them, to neutralize them, even to change them sometimes without being aware of it. It implies that the basic strategy, and I would insist a little on what I mentioned, must come from below, not from above. Fortunately, university bureaucracy is sufficiently indifferent to the academic aspect not to realize what is happening below, and this is basic. That is our first university domain. They are not sensitive to what is happening; furthermore, I dare say that lately they don't care if it goes to the teacher or not, they don't care, as long as the student does not complain. University peace is the peace of the grave: as long as no noise is heard, the university marches on. It is similar to the concept of what a good elementary school teacher is: a good teacher is one who keeps children motionless. Thus, the good principal is one who keeps students and professors motionless. That is why I believe the democratization process has been won, because I think that university administration is not afraid of the academic aspect, but it is afraid of the manifestation of the political aspect, and then it yields and grants in order to neutralize this. This is one of the mechanisms of university corruption that has occurred: the present university professor is not strictly an intellectual worker, because he or she produces and thinks very little and has been corrupted by this mechanism of university adminis-tration that determines when the university is smoothly functioning and when it is functioning poorly. It functions poorly when there is a strike and it functions smoothly when there is apparent peace—that is, when there isn't any boy from the popular high school trying to seize or invade the office of the principal for the tenth time in a week.

I believe that the seizure of power—and when we talk about power and access to power we talk a little in figurative language about the power that surrounds us and not about the central power that rules everything— is not free from the possibility of drafting an academic policy and of having access to the freedom spaces provided by the institution. I think that the three aspects are built together. You do not need first to have power to make an academic policy. To the extent that we make an academic policy, we not only formulate it, but we make an academic policy by practicing it every day. In that sense, it is more powerful.

P. Freire: At this moment I would like to thank Emilio Ribes for something. I am now very pedagogic in the speech, the speech is in me, is dialectical and a few minutes ago my speech was not dialectical, when I said that to me first it was fundamental to win internal power and later do things. Now, what you have said, and I thank you for it, has let me realize that I wasn't dialectical, you in turn were dialectical when you stated that these questions are occurring within a whole province. That is, to the extent that we do and do not simply draft, that we advance toward the seizure of power, we are asserting a certain power. That was what I wanted to thank you for.

We Professors and Students Are the University

E. Ribes: I believe we have fallen into the trap that one almost always falls into with logical speeches when you apply the petition of principle or two different petitions of principle, and we are trying to discuss it as if it were on the same level as categories, and it assumes control based on what it defines to be the first principle to be discussed. We should invest in this process. We have something which does not have university administration, we have the university, because the university is not the dean. All professors and students are the university and the dean is part of the university to the extent that he shares this concept with us. Otherwise he is not the dean; he is an officer, but he is not the dean. I believe that from this point of view we should not stop refuting, criticizing, or even trying to modify the administration. It is important not to leave the administration a land alien and foreign to the academics. I don't think we should basically concentrate on that. The work of the students with the professors implies the making of a political life out of an academic life, which allows us to do our own things, autonomous from the administrators, because the type of professional we are going to make does not have anything to do with the minutes of the University Council [the highest technical council for the schools]. We have been seized by formalism; we believe that a piece of paper rules our destinies and that is false. The graduate that is going to come out of the university, is the one we are going to form. If they cut resources, it is necessary for us to become creative. With the economic crisis we are living through, I don't feel any difference in what I do at the university. I have not been particulary affected, because if I do not obtain a word processor, I use paper and pencil. I don't think we need to depend on a series of devices that originate from frivolity, from instrumentation, and from many other things. We must create a university according to the resources we have. If we have less resources, we do the same but in another way. It's not doing less, it is doing the same but in another way.

This is very important in the sense that if we propose to do it, we can create real power and not formal power. A University Council power is something formal, the power of the schools' technical councils is formal. Real power depends on what is done and not on what is said should be done. University reform is not a formal reform because it appears in the gazette and after it appears in the gazette it is not seen anywhere else, because it does not translate into practical changes. No such reform can occur, but the persons who are guilty if there is no change are us, because we do not change our practices even when a space is formally opened. That is, where we sin for being the opposite of what José Angel Pescador mentioned yesterday. We are pessimistic and skeptical of both the emotional and the cognitive aspects of the university.

I think that an example would illustrate this: we have put to the right the college or associations of professors. The problem of professors is discussed only when we have to decide once again who has the right to be hired and which professors will not be around in another two years, something like a bulletin board or the like. I think we should recover the college of professors. We should organize alternative collegiate ways of evaluating academic work, that convinces those people who do not totally agree with us to perform that work with the daily tasks of the professor's work. The right can affect up to where the university structure allows itself to be affected, but in a way that the professor and students do not realize that what we are proposing concerns what they do, we will always be alien to them, and then it is much more comfortable to be afraid and simply wait until a group of associations who do not ask for or demand anything from them give them something. An academic action policy could facilitate the conquest of a real autonomy in the matter or question of To be able to practice an educational policy once again implies the creation of basic organisms or organizations in the academic life of professors and students, where policy is something that goes hand-in-hand with academics.

P. Freire: I want to thank you for this invitation from the UNAM, which has given me the opportunity to share with you these enriching moments. To me this has been an extraordinary experience that I enjoyed very much. I have participated in seminars of this type in various countries (Germany, Switzerland, England, Brazil, etc.) but I can assure you that the one we have shared these three days is among the most interesting, because of the level of the discussions, the quality of the participants, and the wealth of subjects. I leave very happy to have lived this experience with you, my friends.

M. Escobar: On behalf of the National University of Mexico (UNAM), I want to thank Paulo Freire for being here on this campus. Paulo Freire, a pilgrim of the obvious, is a testimony of revolutionary pedagogy and his praxis is a constant invitation to create and re-create new domains of freedom and to formulate a critique of domesticating pedagogy.

Afterword: Reclaiming Empowerment and Rethinking the Past

A Backdrop

In some ways this dialogue seems to speak from another age. The moment of the Nicaraguan Revolution, recognized in the final stages of the dialogue, has passed. More profoundly, the very notion of socialist revolutions, as we conceived and knew them, seems already to belong to a quite different time.

A more innocent time? Maybe. Certainly a time when problems, answers, and agendas often appeared more simple. More linear. More certain, perhaps. Just ten years ago, the lines dividing the politically correct from the politically incorrect seemed to have been drawn with remarkable clarity. At least, this is how it looked from self-professed politically correct standpoints.

For many of us who inhabited schools, departments, or faculties in the academy, the contours of battle appeared self-evident and the strategies obvious. We must, we thought, win the recruiting and curriculum battles and build "our side" by ensuring the "right" appointments are made and the "right" courses put in place.

Sometimes "we" won the battles and achieved numerical majorities. Thus empowered we changed courses and programs. But in many such cases we lost what was most important: *revolutionary* vision and will. We operated unwittingly, but effectively, to close down the dialectic. We mistook "revolutionary progress" for "surrounding ourselves with kindred spirits." The price was high. Debate became stunted: when you have the numbers why *argue* for your choice? Slogans often seemed to be enough.

Recognizing liberal tolerance for the sham it is, we too often felt justified in abandoning tolerance altogether. Strike two against debate, against *revolutionary* change. Authentic revolutionary change, being dialectical, presupposes tolerance. It presupposes debate. Without debate we might, indeed, hold fast to our "truth." But we do so at the cost of refusing to expose it to the risk of challenge. Ironically, this risk has traditionally defined the ethos and raison d'être of the academy and possibly remains the academy's strongest justification and basis for survival.

Only through continual recommitment to the values and practices of debate and tolerance on the part of its members can the university maintain its historical and revolutionary viability. Only by living with risk and exposing our "truths" to the most rigorous self criticism and critical scrutiny of others can we, as progressive academics, keep alive the possibility of contributing to authentic revolutionary change.

In reminding us of this necessary dialectical truth, the dialogue recorded in this volume strikes a profoundly contemporary note—notwithstanding the demise of the Nicaraguan Revolution and the emergence of a longer shadow that has fast fallen on faith in grand narratives of deliverance. The many themes traversed in dialogue by Paulo Freire and the group of academics from UNAM, around their focus on constructing education for liberation in a university setting, provide fruitful stimuli for our ongoing development as historical subjects in quest of emancipation and justice for all.

One theme in particular resonates with a concern that seems to me very important right now. It has to do with struggle for symbolic power and the danger of liberating concepts of education losing their vital force. Alfredo Fernández captures this point and its significance very nicely in the dialogue:

[T]he dominating class, through its hegemony in [the] existing structure, recuperates the liberating concepts of education and immediately transforms them into empty terminology, void of useful meanings and strength as ideas. . . [They] . . . become only words. . . always [lacking] the expected content. They await re-creation of their content through the political practice of liberating education.[1]

In response, Paulo Freire asserts the value of undertaking "a type of investigation among ourselves of groups of concepts that have become depleted, in order to experience and revive them, really putting them in practice."[2]

This is a worthy and timely challenge. I want to begin addressing it here in a manner that celebrates the call to subject our "truths" to the risk of scrutiny. In what follows I will focus on what I see as depletion of the concept of 'empowerment' through indiscriminate and unreflective use. Empowerment talk has become widespread recently among educators who espouse commitment to ideals of 'emancipation', 'liberation', 'autonomy', 'equality', 'social justice', and the like.

A Case in Point

Empowerment is, I believe, in danger of losing its theoretical and practical force. This is partly a function of what participants in the dialogue identify as the capacity of "the dominant class" to recuperate concepts like empowerment, adapt them to social demands, and thereby transform them into so much "hollow, nominal, and empty terminology." Concha Delgado-Gaitan relates her initial resistance to using empowerment as the central analytic and explanatory construct in her study of education in a southern Californian migrant community precisely to the fact that it has "been used to mean the act of showing people how to work within a system from the perspective of the people in power."[3]

At the same time, however, educational theorists and practitioners committed to the liberatory ideal of authentic education have themselves contributed to devaluing the currency of empowerment. We have done so in two main ways.

We have often unintentionally diminished the original value of empowerment by using it "to *name* the space where theoretical work is needed rather than to fill that space."[4] Such "promiscuous use [of empowerment] in exercises of theoretical painting by numbers" may well serve "to preclude the need for more theoretical work" when, in fact, such work is much needed.[5]

The second way in which liberatory educators have "helped" reduce empowerment to hollow, nominal, and empty terminology is by invoking it *ad nauseum* as some kind of educational magic bullet. We often assume that the meaning and "credentials" of empowerment are self-evident and generally accepted, and believe that simply injecting the term into educational discourse will produce a strategy for solving personal and collective educational problems and overcoming existing barriers to 'emancipation' and 'equity'.

Before empowerment becomes hopelessly depleted, we would do well to take up Freire's challenge and subject it to "a kind of investigation," in order to "experience and revive" it and "put it into practice."

Conceptual Issues

Let me begin by drawing on conceptual work done some years ago in social philosophy on the concept of freedom. Building on earlier efforts by Maurice Cranston and Gerald MacCallum, Joel Feinberg cautions that claims about freedom are often elliptical, or abbreviated.[6] For example, when appeals are made to "economic freedom" as a policy ideal, we need to know whether the appellants mean freedom of the economy to operate according to market forces untrammelled by government intervention; or the freedom of individuals to meet their material needs by having access to adequate economic resources; or something else again. Feinberg endorses Cranston's claim that we should "call for the full version of all such abbreviated slogans', otherwise we don't know what we are supporting, demanding, or trying to bring about.[7]

According to Feinberg's analysis, which remains the best I have seen for dealing with freedom as a social concept, 'freedom' expresses a relation among three variables: a subject, a constraint, and an outcome. Providing a full account of statements involving freedom requires specifying *who* or *what* is free (or unfree); *from what* they are free (or unfree); and what it is that they are free (or unfree) *to do, be, have, become,* and so on. Cashing out conceptually elliptical statements about freedom will normally involve filling in "blanks" in a triadic schema, thus:

_____ is free from _____ to do, be, have, etc. _____.[8]

Many statements about empowerment are similarly elliptical, although they typically entail at least *four* variables. Elucidating such statements calls for specifying: (1) the *subject* of empowerment; (2) the power *structures* in relation to which, or in opposition to which, a person or group is being empowered; (3) the *processes* or *"qualities"* through or by which empowerment occurs; and (4) the *ends* or *outcomes* of being thus empowered.

That is, claims about empowerment must specify values for A–D in a schema of the form:

A (the subject) is empowered in respect of **B** (some aspect of the discursive structuring of power) by/through **C** (a process or quality) such that **D** (a valued end or outcome) ensues.

Very real advantages flow from taking the conceptual demands of empowerment seriously. There is far more at stake here than mere semantics or linguistic pedantry. The more closely and clearly we specify particular learner-subjects, the more likely we are to identify forms and processes of power that limit their options within everyday settings and to envisage or negotiate learning processes and outcomes in line with the ends we seek. Similarly, the better our theory is of how power is produced and distributed, the more we will understand the varying circumstances and aspirations of different learners and the better informed will be the means and processes employed toward (negotiated) learning outcomes.

It is one thing to advance a conceptual model and assert claims for its potential usefulness in focusing pedagogical activity; it is another, however, to demonstrate its usefulness by means of examples and creative applications. I will try to do this by reviewing an account I myself advanced of an instance of "empowering literacy."[9]

A Fit Case for Treatment:
"Literacy and Running Your Life"

Numerous writers have observed that adult literacy initiatives can serve either "to domesticate and further subordinate" or "to increase the autonomy and social standing" of previously illiterate persons.[10] I subscribe to this view and over several years now have tried to amplify it and to identify cases where adult literacy initiatives have enhanced the autonomy and social standing of learners.

On the basis of observations and interviews gathered over a year of living with a group of Nicaraguan peasants immediately prior to the demise of the revolution, I published an account of empirical conditions under which a strictly limited functional literacy had what I saw as *empowering* consequences. The notion of empowerment provided the conceptual focus for "Literacy and Running Your Life." It was not, however, subjected to any rigorous analytic or theoretical treatment. Rather, in the manner denounced by Dale, "empowerment" was used to *name* rather than to *fill* a space where theoretical work was required. The price of this omission became evident to me during subsequent visits to the San José cooperative after the electoral defeat of the Sandinista government in February 1990.

In the Beginning

It was clear to the architects of Nicaragua's National Literacy Crusade of 1980 (CNA) and the subsequent program of Popular Basic Education for Adults (PBEA) that achieving the broad educational and social goals laid down was not simply a matter of what was done *within* these programmes. Wider changes would have to be made that actually stimulated confidence among learners and provided an ongoing basis and context for practicing and refining literacy, generating conditions whereby literacy skills could become an integral part of an enhanced life and active participation in processes of social and political change.[11]

Among those policies and reforms enacted since 1979 that had consequences for basic literacy within the round of daily routines was a government initiative to encourage cooperative forms of economic production. During the early 1980s a variety of cooperative forms emerged, with generous credit and nonfinancial incentives made available by government. Encouragement to establish cooperative ventures engendered a new opportunity for previously underemployed and otherwise economically marginal Nicaraguans to secure steady paid work, and to experience responsibility for and control over the work process. The consequent demands imposed on cooperative members to administer their enterprise had obvious implications for literacy. Many of those who formed or joined cooperatives, and accepted positions of administrative responsibility within them, were newly and minimally literate "graduates" of the CNA and/or PBEA.

Do You Know the Way to San José?

San José is a light-industrial manufacturing cooperative set in a traditionally agricultural community thirty kilometers from Managua. It was established by a group of peasants for whom underemployment and economic insecurity had been the norm throughout their adult lives. San José's founders attribute the stimulus to form a cooperative to government policies—without which the idea would not have occurred to them. Nine men and six women subsequently joined, contributing what meagre capital they could muster to establish a base for their labor-intensive enterprise. Literacy levels among members are low, with the women's print competency being rather higher on average than the men's. The women average at least a second-grade-level school education. They read texts like newspapers and Bible-study booklets reasonably fluently, although their writing is labored.

Manufacturing production commenced in the mid 1980s with very simple brooms made from a species of wheat—the wheat bristles being wired to handles "rounded" manually, with wire also being used to "stitch" the bristles into shape. By 1989 production had diversified, but remained labor intensive across the board. Products included mop heads made of plaited cotton (*mechas*), attachments for *mechas* (a wooden handle and a steel holding mechanism) called *lampazos*, a range of nylon-bristled brushes and brooms, and a simple but highly efficient hand pump for use on wells.

There was a complex division of labor that, in the final analysis, was gender based. Briefly, women worked making *mechas* and inserting bristles into nylon brushes. Men made *lampazos*, built pumps, and produced the wooden housings for brushes and brooms as well as broom handles. This gendered division of labor notwithstanding, some inroads had seemingly been made at San José into traditional notions and practices associated with *machismo*. On one occasion, when the supply of cotton dried up temporarily, the cooperative discussed the economic situations of Luisa and Isabel and supported their requests to continue earning by working on pump production until there was more cotton. They worked a few days on tasks but returned to unpaid domestic chores before new cotton supplies arrived.

Considering San José's infrastructure, the scale and efficiency of production was impressive. Vendors from city markets collected *lampazos* in lots of 500. On a good day 450 or more *mechas* were produced and bagged: these were a lucrative product. From the outset the cooperative members had invested a proportion of their profits into developing the enterprise. Most families had built permanent material dwellings from income, purchasing materials as they could afford them and commencing construction once all the necessities had been acquired. These homes stand out in the community in terms of size, quality, and amenities. The children were all in school, the older ones attending the *colegio* in Managua. Most intended to continue onto university or other tertiary institutions. Such factors indicated a quite remarkable change in life quality over a five-year period.

By late 1988 the scale and sophistication of production was straining the educational level of members to breaking point. On one side there were the demands of keeping the books, doing the banking, maintaining records, paying taxes, and so on. In addition, however, there was an obvious need to attain a greater degree of mastery over the production process itself in the midst of hyperinflation and ever-changing prices. Prices of completed products had to reflect the real prices paid for materials, and careful oversight of each step in production was needed to prevent losses creeping in at any point.

Administration had been easier at first, when production was on a smaller scale and was less diverse and when products were less complex. Initially, San José had limited local access to an accountant. This had provided the minimum support necessary to meet administrative needs. But when the accountant left the district, the load fell formally on the cooperative's treasurer, Isabel.

Isabel had learned to read and write in the 1980 crusade and had continued through three levels of adult education until classes ceased in the neighborhood. By

agrarian reform, health campaigns, a new labor code] and spearheaded the creation of structures and processes [e.g., mass organizations, channels of dialogue between people and leadership, etc.] which helped imbue popular literacy with real empowering effect, and gave the masses grounds for believing that their lives could be improved through their own involvement."[16]

5. "[During Nicaragua's revolutionary years] case upon case reveals commitment and ingenuity on the part of revolutionary leaders and those spearheading the mass organisations to create conditions whereby literacy—albeit of a most rudimentary and technically flawed form—could become an instrument of genuine empowerment for individuals and groups within the key spheres of their daily lives."[17]

Nothing beyond these claims was advanced by way of analyzing or defining "empowerment" more explicitly. At most, empirical evidence was provided for key claims that *presupposed* the term. The question of how the challenge of empowering marginalized people to tackle their most pressing daily concerns was taken up inside the CNA and EPB [Educación Popular Básica] is a typical example. This was addressed by noting pedagogical attempts to expose oppressive ideologies, mentioning the close links established between educational content and everyday experience, and documenting simple but ingenious means used to engage learners in acting materially on the words and themes around which lessons were built. Hence "as projects [e.g., building latrines, creating a water supply, constructing houses and schools] unfolded and were completed, participants actually *experienced* . . . agency within the act of coming to see the possibility and importance of becoming literate historical agents."[18]

Following the description of economic activity in San José, and in accordance with that description as framed around key claims already noted, two main conclusions were drawn.

First, the case study of literacy and daily life in San José "illustrates the important place literacy can and does play in the process of people assuming greater control in running their daily lives and improving their quality and experience of life as a consequence."

Second, the case study "suggests that sympathetic and constructive support for even the most basic literacy skills is integral to realising the empowering potential of being able to read and write, when that support is conceived in accordance with democratic and emancipatory goals."[19]

Cause for Pause: San José, January 1992

The Sandinista government fell in February 1990. When I returned briefly to San José in January 1992 I was told of major changes to the cooperative's activities.

Cotton production nationally had fallen dramatically, and no cotton for *mecha* production had been available for several months. There was no foreseeable change in that situation. Previous protections for local products had been removed, opening the market to imported lines that were cheaper and of higher quality than local variants. San José's nylon brushes and brooms were casualties here. Finally, the hand pumps developed and produced on the cooperative as a pilot project had proved highly popular nationwide. Project personnel found cheaper and higher quality sources of supply than could be managed at San José.

That is, each of the income earning activities of 1989 had either disappeared or else had been seriously undermined by January 1992, at which time production was restricted to two lines. First, an imported lathe financed by an international development project was being used to convert rough-sawn timber into high-quality handles for brooms and mops. Profits on this line were good, although the market was finite. Handles sold for twice the cost of the timber. The machine could, however, with the unskilled labor of one person, produce more in a day than might be sold in a month.

The other line was especially interesting. The cooperative had returned to where it began, producing wheat-bristled brooms of the same original design and for which there remained a traditional market. Cooperative members were using land to grow the appropriate species of wheat, rather then cropping *yuca, trigo* (sorgum), rice, and maize, as they had in 1989. The original homemade "machines," built in 1984 to shape and hold bristles and to unwind the wire for stitching, were back in use. In a stunning juxtaposition, the imported lathe provided their technological complement, fashioning high-quality handles for these homely brooms.

In summary, the women were out of paid work and the men were on severely reduced work. At least two men had left the cooperative: one to produce carbon for sale in the city, the other to clean warehouses in Los Angeles. Sufficient evidence was available from this brief visit to cast severe doubts on the adequacy of my initial account of literacy and empowerment.

Improving the Treatment: "Investigation, Experiencing, and Reviving Depleted Concepts"

'Literacy and Running Your Life' functions at the level of *generalized* talk about literacy and empowerment. The account *could* be made a little more specific, so far as empowerment talk is concerned, within its original frame by elaborating certain points. For example:

1. San José's members had sufficient command of print to be able to process and convey the minimum information requirements for establishing and maintaining a legally constituted cooperative.

2. The cooperative institutionalized a logic of "the power of numbers" in pursuit of economic survival and enhancement, in place of the more typical but atomized approach of individuals trying to "make it on their own." The act of combining resources generated the power of a capital base. From this base, members sought—with good success—to enhance their economic power through accumulating profits and exercising control over the use of those profits (for example, in further developing infrastructure to further enhance profitability).

3. Enhanced economic power led to a greatly increased level of material life—improved housing, sanitation, clothing, education—for families in the cooperative.

4. In a context that provided appropriate forms of educational support, the literacy base of members allowed them to access knowledge and techniques conducive to improving the efficiency and viability of their enterprise. That is, under highly supportive conditions, the literacy they possessed gave them access to the power afforded by further knowledge—including new literacies, such as elementary accounting and keeping records—that presupposed and was mediated by print.

5. Being literate contributed to cooperative members feeling more confident about acting, and acting

more confidently, publicly as well as inside the enterprise. This encouraged them to seek access to resources that could promote their interests further and to participate within a range of institutional structures and settings in which they experienced, collectively and as individuals, the discursive production and distribution of different forms of *power*. These included the power to make decisions, to frame and solve problems, to determine rules and procedures, to negotiate, as well as the power of (privileged) access to resources and benefits made available only to cooperatives, and so on.

Such additions might refine and shore up somewhat the case developed within the original conceptual and theoretical framework. The problem is, however, that even when bolstered in this way the framework itself remains unduly limited and limiting. It is simply not sharp enough to focus attention on some of the most important aspects of the situations that confronted members of San José. Worse still, in many respects it encourages oversimplification and distortion.

Applying the conceptual schema of empowerment developed earlier allows much greater specificity, as well as opening up additional issues for analysis. By way of conclusion, let me relate the schema to my original account and note some of the points at which it helps avoid distortion, positively enhances accuracy, and opens up discussion along potentially fruitful lines.

Putting More Power into Empowerment

In the original account the **A** variable is effectively assumed to apply to cooperative members generally and collectively. The 1992 situation, however, suggests that at the very least a distinction ought to be drawn between men and women, since with the cut back in production men alone were left earning. This effectively confirmed their status as breadwinners, notwithstanding the fact that the work being done could have been performed equally well by either gender. Appealing to the schema, rather then engaging in more generalized talk of empowerment, helps focus attention on finer grained distinctions and analysis here. In doing so it unmasks an important issue that was glossed to the point of distortion in the original, namely, the extent to which traditional assumptions and practices pertaining to gender and work lived on.

The **B** variable applies most obviously to structures of economic activity. More specifically, literacy was integral to wider processes and relations through which the members of San José could operate as small scale *entrepreneurial capitalists*. They acquired power to control the distribution and use of profit, power to determine tasks, power to ensure their own employment and the conditions of their employment to a far greater extent than local landless laborers and housebound women: which is what these people *were* before establishing San José. To this extent, the **B** variable allows us to focus attention on the nature and discursive production of *economic* power—its relational and structural characteristics—within a simple form of (entrepreneurial) *capitalist accumulation*. This permits a much finer grained account of the empowering significance of literacy than afforded by the original framework, calling for description and analysis of how print enters the discourse of economic production under these particular conditions.

At the same time we would be alerted to actual and potential *limits* to empowerment inherent in discourses of capitalism; for example, dependence on markets and vulnerability to market shifts; constraints imposed by price-fixing mechanisms, the wider policy contexts within which one operates, and so on. These are important matters, as we will see below, that were largely masked within the original under-conceptualized framework.

The **B** variable could also be opened up along other fronts, such as the structures by which 'powerful' knowledge is controlled and/or operated. The example of the "cooperative doctor" illustrates peasant producers being enabled to access—and, subsequently, produce for themselves—knowledge of an otherwise specialized/expert kind. This is knowledge that has real power for generating economic options, higher levels of profit, and for retaining control over the integrity of one's enterprise. In other contexts, such knowledge might be seen as the preserve of consultants. This establishes a relation of dependence between those needing the service and those providing it. Changing the structural conditions of access to and control of such knowledge speaks loudly to an important form of empowerment.

The **C** variable directs attention to processes by which, and qualities through which, cooperative members took on new positions in relation to the discursive production and allocation of power. Key *processes* include diverse policies and programs implemented by the Sandinista government. These extend from the literacy and adult education programs that "literated" people like Isabel in the first place, to the support structures and networks for cooperatives, and the various incentives and subsidies that stretched to the maximum the capital base and investments of new cooperative producers. From another angle, literacy itself can be seen as a *quality* that helped San José's members gain admittance to new relationships to power as well as to new levels of knowledge and technique.

The **D** (or **outcome**) variable ranges over improved standards of living, enhanced experience of control, a stronger sense of economic security, higher levels of personal fulfillment, and so on. It should also be pointed out—and the "empowerment schema" calls attention to this in a way that the original framework could not—that in the case of San José a most important outcome consisted in the "space" members of the cooperative could generate through their (reconstituted) activities and achievements from which to extend benefits of many kinds to the wider community. The benefits were many and varied. They extended from making the factory available for community meetings, to transporting sick neighbors to the hospital, to using their machinery and timber to build seating for the church or coffins for dead infants—always at no cost and with no expectation of reciprocity or indebtedness. At another level, San José modelled *possibility*. The stature of its members was marked within the wider community. They were key players in a range of discursive sites, in many respects exemplifying the "new kinds of Nicaraguans" envisioned in the ideal of *Sandinismo*.

Much more, of course, could be said: by way of identifying still other interpretive and elaborative possibilites as well as by way of critique of my original account of literacy for empowerment inside the Nicaraguan Revolution. Further reflections must, however, await fresh opportunities to investigate, experience, and revive the diminished—but not yet entirely depleted—conceptual terrain of empowerment. It remains here only to recognize the inherently relative nature of empowerment and the extent to which particular *subjects of empowerment* may yet remain marginal and disempowered in significant respects. Three aspects occur with regard to San José.

The position of women vis-à-vis men should be explored. First, my underdeveloped original conception of empowerment was in effect gender blind. The relatively bouyant situation I observed in 1989, one in which the women seemingly participated on more-or-less equal terms with men, did not caution closer critical attention to the "gendering" of empowerment within the universe of San José. Moreover, the impressive presence of Isabel (as constructed through my limited interpretive frame) was an added distraction. The situation I observed in 1992, however, points inescapably to arrangements at San José having empowered men over women in important respects.

Second, the cooperative experienced a quite profound setback following the change of government and the revoking of Sandinista economic policies that privileged and protected cooperatives. San José's members experienced enhanced power *within* particular discursive and policy arrangements established under the Sandinista regime, deriving improved conditions and other benefits as a consequence. The power to create and preserve such conditions and benefits *outside* of these discursive and policy arrangements, however, remained largely *beyond* the cooperative's members. The extent to which this was true became obvious when the revolution finally fell. This is in no way to demean the efforts and achievements either of the cooperative members or of the revolutionary government and its supporters. Both were impressive within their contexts. It is simply to observe the wide horizons and multiple dimensions of power and, hence, of empowerment.

Finally—and related to the previous point—it is important to observe a distinction between internal and external, or *personal* and *institutional*, dimensions of empowerment in relation to literacy. Conceived in terms of personal competencies, the literacy of San José's members was and remained fragile, vulnerable. Outside of sympathetically supportive arrangements, it could have little currency.

The importance of establishing policies that lend the greatest enabling effect to even the most rudimentary forms of literacy, thereby rendering them (more) functional, was a key message in "Literacy and Running Your Life." This speaks to external-institutional dimensions of empowerment through literacy. They are crucially important but are not, on their own, sufficient. Outside of radical politics of democracy the functional-making attributes of supportive institutional arrangements cannot be counted on.

As Allan Luke has often remarked, "we need to put teeth into empowering literacy." This, as he makes clear, involves addressing *internal* as well as external dimensions, by maximizing learners' technical and critical-analytic competencies with print.[20]

By attending to both dimensions, more direct and abiding links between literacy and empowerment can be established, ones that outlive changes of regime and political direction. Such links, as it happens, are the first fruits of a truly liberating education.

Postscript

We have come full circle and end as Gilberto Guevara began, with questions and reflections focused on power and the role liberatory education may play within a praxis that transforms the ways power is produced, re-produced, and distributed socially.

Just as education cannot be the *lever* for social transformation,[21] neither can it be sufficient on its own to *maintain* programs of democratic social change that are already underway. All the liberatory pedagogy in the world cannot withstand the sapping undermining impact of imperialist sabotage in Contra garb.

Equally, however, the full potential of the role education *can* play within a larger praxis of social change will only be realized to the extent that we understand power intimately—which implies understanding power as a discursive production—and become capable of *reinventing* it in educational contexts.

For all the obvious surface differences evident in daily life and educational practice between the Nicaraguan countryside, the Mexican academy, and the schools and communities of the so-called First World; and between transition societies like Nicaragua 1979–90 and "pre-revolutionary" societies; the "depth grammars" are remarkably similar, so far as power and its reinvention are concerned.

Here we may recall Paulo Freire's words in the opening pages,[22] where he says that the revolution-in-power has (still) to create a new society and a new education. A new society cannot appear by decree, but must "appear before *history*." This calls for reinventing power, dialectically, in and through education, within and without education. The new education—of and for the new society—is simultaneously a dimension of the overall praxis of reinventing social power *and* an outcome of this larger reinvention of power.

This came home to me most graphically during many evenings in 1989 when I sat among locals in Monte

Fresco in dirt-floored *salas*, or stood in dusty yards, watching Brazilian soap opera extravaganzas on small black-and-white television screens. In such settings the Nicaraguan Revolution met the communications revolution head on in the postmodern battle for subjectivities and identities. Quite simply, the fledgling new education in the new Nicaragua was, so far as I could tell, poorly placed to counteract the ideological and identity-constitutive impact of the entertainment fare provided by Sandinista television.

The response made by locals to my despair at this cultural invasion—that there was no other entertainment available in the countryside, and that they worked hard and deserved some vicarious diversion—was one I could not counter. Yet, in the spaces between the pulsating portrayal of the fantastical desires and passions of urban Brazilian glitterati by night, and the careful creation of handmade nuts and bolts for *lampazos* by day, was wrought a massive decentering of subjective experience and institutional life and, I believe, a considerable displacement of revolutionary political potential.

It is impossible to overestimate the implications for the politics of reinventing power of such quintessentially postmodern processes and "events," which now are manufactured and managed on a global scale. Everywhere they prompt deep and complex questions bearing on the prospects for societywide movements of social change aimed at more equitable discursive productions of power, opportunity, and well-being.

Many of these questions, including the most important, have been raised in the dialogue recorded in this book. They range from questions about the role of political parties and the mobilizing potential of new social movements to issues of how best to construct critical pedagogies that respect the integrity of learners, yet enable them to resist and transcend the fragmenting and depoliticizing tendencies of contemporary forms of meaning making and the meanings that are made and lived thereby.

The call to liberation is, precisely, a call to understand and reinvent power. This quest is by no means exhausted in and through dialogue that critiques domesticating pedagogy and seeks to transform it. Such dialogue is, however, of the essence.

Colin Lankshear
Queensland, Australia

Notes

Foreword

1. Benita Parry, "A Critique Mishandled" (*Social Text* 35, 1993, pp. 121–33), p. 130.

2. Andrew Ross, *No Respect: Intellectuals and Popular Culture* (New York and London: Routledge, 1989), p. 129.

3. Ross, *No Respect*, ibid.

4. Ross, *No Respect*, ibid.

5. Joe Kincheloe and Peter McLaren, "You Can't Get to the Emerald City from Here: Rethinking Critical Theory and Qualitative Research," in Norm K. Denzin and Yvonna S. Lincoln, eds., *Handbook of Qualitative Research* (Newbury Park, Calif.: Sage Publications, in press).

6. Jim Gee, "Postmodernism and Literacies," in Colin Lanshear and Peter McLaren, eds., *Critical Literacy: Politics, Praxis, and the Postmodern* (Albany, N.Y.: SUNY Press, 1993), pp. 271–96.

7. Jim Berlin, "Literacy, Pedagogy, and English Studies: Postmodern Connections," in Colin Lanshear and Peter McLaren, eds., *Critical Literacy: Politics, Praxis, and the Postmodern* (Albany, N.Y.: SUNY Press, 1993), pp. 247–70.

8. Henry Giroux, *Border Crossings* (New York: Routledge, 1993).

9. Peter McLaren and Peter Leonard, eds., *Paulo Freire: A Critical Encounter* (London and New York: Routledge, 1993).

10. Peter McLaren and Colin Lankshear, eds., *Politics of Liberation: Paths from Freire* (London and New York: Routledge, in press).

11. Jésus Martíin-Barbero, *Communication, Culture and Hegemony: From Media to Meditation* (London: Sage Publications, 1992); Peter McLaren, "Collisions with Otherness: Multiculturalism, the Politics of Difference, and the Ethnographer as Nomad" (*The American Journal of Semiotics* 9, nos. 2–3, 1992, pp. 121–48.

12. Sande Cohen, *Academia and the Luster of Capital* (Minneapolis: University of Minnesota Press, 1993), p. 154 (italics original).

13. Cohen, *Academia*, p. 3.

14. Cohen, *Academia*, p. 68.

15. Cohen, *Academia*, p. 114.

16, Cohen, *Academia*, p. 67.

17. Cohen, *Academia*, p. 70.

18. Cohen, *Academia*, p. 70.

19. Cohen, *Academia*, p. 72.

20. Cohen, *Academia*, p. 73.

21. Cohen, *Academia*, p. 113.

22. Cohen, *Academia*, p. 118.

23. Cohen, *Academia*, p. 119.

24. Gaurav Desai, "The Invention of Invention" (*Cultural Critique* 24, 1993, pp. 119–42), p. 137.

25. Desai, "Invention of Invention," ibid.

26. Jim Merod, *The Political Responsibility of the Critic* (Ithaca: Cornell University Press, 1987), p. 188.

27. Merod, *Political Responsibility*, p. 191.

28. Homi K. Bhabha, *Nation and Narration* (London and New York: Routledge, 1990), p. 314.

29. Bhabha, *Nation and Narration*, p. 315.

30. Bhabha, *Nation and Narration*, p. 314.

31. Bhabha, *Nation and Narration*, p. 314.

32. Bhabha, *Nation and Narration*, p. 315.

33. Bhabha, *Nation and Narration*, p. 316.

34. Peter Hitchcock, *Dialogics of the Oppressed* (Minneapolis: University of Minnesota Press, 1993).

35. Joan W. Scott, "Experience" in Judith Butler and Joan W. Scott, eds., *Feminists Theorize the Political* (New York and London: Routledge, 1992), p. 34.

36. bell hooks and Cornel West, *Breaking Bread: Insurgent Black Intellectual Life* (Boston: South End Press, 1991), p. 137.

37. hooks and West, *Breaking Bread*, p. 137.

38. hooks and West, *Breaking Bread*, p. 142.

39. hooks and West, *Breaking Bread*, p. 138.

40. hooks and West, *Breaking Bread*, p. 140.

41. hooks and West, *Breaking Bread*, p. 140.

42. hooks and West, *Breaking Bread*, p. 141.

43. hooks and West, *Breaking Bread*, p. 142.

44. hooks and West, *Breaking Bread*, p. 143.

45. hooks and West, *Breaking Bread*, p. 152.

46. hooks and West, *Breaking Bread*, p. 157.

47. hooks and West, *Breaking Bread*, p. 158.

48. hooks and West, *Breaking Bread*, p. 160.

49. Samir Amin, *Eurocentrism* (New York: Monthly Review Press, 1989), p. 114.

Introduction

1. This sections draws from Carlos Alberto Torres, "La Educación Superior en América Latina: De la Reforma de 1918 al Ajuste Estructural de los Noventas." Keynote address to the International Symposium on Perspectives of the University Curricuium in the XXI Century. Faculty of Sciences of Education, National University of Entre Rios, Paraná, Argentina, August 24–27, 1992.

2. These changes in the patterns of state-society relationships are commonplace in the social historiography of Latin America. For classic examples of historical analysis following this tradition, see Tulio Halperin Donghi, *Histórica Contemporánea de América Latina* (Madrid: Alianza Editorial, 1969); Osvaldo Sunkel and Pedro Paz, *El Subdesarrollo Latinoamericano y la Teoría del Desarrollo* (Mexico: Siglo XXI, 1970); Eduardo P. Archetti, Paul Cammarck, and Bryan Roberts (editors), *Sociology of "Developing Societies": Latin America* (Houndmills, Basinstoke and London: Macmillan, 1987); and Helio Jaguaribe, Aldo Ferrer, Miguel S. Wionczek, and Theotonio Dos Santos, *La Dependencia político-Económica de América Latina* (Mexico: Siglo XXI, 1970). For a reappraisal of this literature, see the extensive and documented study of Ruth Berins Collier and David Collier, *Shaping the Political Arena: Critical Junctures, the Labor Movement, and Regime Dynamics in Latin America* (Princeton, N.J.: Princeton University Press, 1991).

3. See the insightful work of Atilio A. Boron: "The Formation and Crisis of the Olisarchical State in Argentina, 1880–1930" (Ph.D. dissertation, Harvard University, 1976).

4. Carlos Alberto Torres, *The Church, Society and Hegemony: A Critical Sociology of Religion in Latin America,* transl. by Richard Young (Westport, Conn. and London: Praeger, 1992).

5. Collier and Collier, *Shaping the Political Arena.* pp. 15–20.

6. See Carlos Alberto Torres, "Argentina." In Philip G. Altbach, ed., *International Higher Education: An Encyclopedia* (New York and London: Garland, 1991), vol. 2, pp. 869–83.

7. International Student Conference by the Coordinating Secretariat of the Nation al Unions of Students on University Reform in Latin America, Leiden, the Netherlands 1959.

8. Gilbert Guevara-Niebla, *El Saber y el Poder* (Culiacán, Sinaloa: Universidade de Sinaloa, 1986).

9. Raúl Atria, Eduardo Acuña, et al., "El Estado de la Investigación Tipológica Acerca de la Universidad en América Latina." In *La Universidad Latinoamericana: Enfoques Tipológicos,* p. 31.

10. José Joaquín Brunner," Invessgación Científica y Educación Superior en América Latina" (Santiago de Chile: FLACSO, Documento de Trabajo 452, June 1990), p. 2. Brunner qualifies this observation in another work in which he indicates that because of the state's role as financer, the investment in development and research from 1970 to 1980 went from $500 million to $3,500. See J. J. Brunner, "Higher Education and the Formation of the Professional in Latin America" (Santiago de Chile: FLACSO, Documento de Trabajo 380, August, 1988), p. 15.

11. In the writing of this section the following monoraphs by José Joaquín Brunner have been particularly useful: "La Educación Superior y la Formación Professional en América Latina" (Santiago de Chile: FLACSO, Documento de Trabajo

381, September, 1988); "Educación Superior y Cultura en América Latina: Función y organización" (Santiago de Chile: FLACSO, Documento de Trabajo 412, July, 1989); "Gobierno Universitario: Elementos de análisis y Discusión" (Santiago de Chile: FLACSO, Documento de Trabajo 414, July, 1989); "Educación Superior y Ciencia: Chile en Perspectiva Internactional Comparada" (Santiago de Chile: FLACSO, Documento de Trabajo 447, May, 1990); "Investigación Científica y educación Superior en América Latina" (Santiago de Chile: FLACSO, Documento de Trabajo 452, June, 1990).

12. The new theoretical perspective in sociology has been introduced in the United States in the last decade. Neo-structural functionalism is the product of a group of American scholars, the majority of them sociologists, who have questioned some of the analytical and methodological premises of Talcott Parsons, but who have conserved to a large extent, his explicative structure, for example, notions of structural differentiation and systemic specialization. Among the most noteworthy representative of this perspective are the works of Jeffrey Alexander; the latest works of Neil Smelser; and in the realm of higher education, the last work of Burton Clark, who has conducted a number of case studies, as well as historical analysis. For a systematic presentation and critical discusion of this tendency, see Raymond A. Morrow and Carlos Albert Torres, "Social Theory and Education," manuscript, 1992. For a comparative analysis (or map) of neo-functionalism in the context of comparative education, see Rolland Paulston "Mapping Paradigms ad Theories in Comparative Education," paper presented at the Comparative and International Education Society annual meeting, Annapolis, Maryland, March, 1992.

13. Of the long list of works by Burton R. Clark see *The Academic Life: Small Words, Different Worlds* (Princeton, N.J.: Carnegie Foundation for the Advancement of Teaching, 1987) and *The Higher Education System: Academic Organization in Cross-National Perspective* (Berkeley, Los Angeles, and London: University of California Press, 1983).

381, September, 1988); "Educación Superior y Cultura en América Latina: Función y organización" (Santiago de Chile: FLACSO, Documento de Trabajo 412, July, 1989); "Gobierno Universitario: Elementos de análisis y Discusión" (Santiago de Chile: FLACSO, Documento de Trabajo 414, July, 1989); "Educación Superior y Ciencia: Chile en Perspectiva Internactional Comparada" (Santiago de Chile: FLACSO, Documento de Trabajo 447, May, 1990); "Investigación Científica y educación Superior en América Latina" (Santiago de Chile: FLACSO, Documento de Trabajo 452, June, 1990).

12. The new theoretical perspective in sociology has been introduced in the United States in the last decade. Neo–structural functionalism is the product of a group of American scholars, the majority of them sociologists, who have questioned some of the analytical and methodological premises of Talcott Parsons, but who have conserved to a large extent, his explicative structure, for example, notions of structural differentiation and systemic specialization. Among the most note-worthy representative of this perspective are the works of Jeffrey Alexander; the latest works of Neil Smelser; and in the realm of higher education, the last work of Burton Clark, who has conducted a number of case studies, as well as historical analysis. For a systematic presentation and critical discusion of this tendency, see Raymond A. Morrow and Carlos Albert Torres, "Social Theory and Education," manuscript, 1992. For a comparative analysis (or map) of neo-functionalism in the context of comparative education, see Rolland Paulston "Mapping Paradigms ad Theories in Comparative Education," paper presented at the Comparative and International Education Society annual meeting, Annapolis, Maryland, March, 1992.

13. Of the long list of works by Burton R. Clark see *The Academic Life: Small Words, Different Worlds* (Princeton, N.J.: Carnegie Foundation for the Advancement of Teaching, 1987) and *The Higher Education System: Academic Organization in Cross-National Perspective* (Berkeley, Los Angeles, and London: University of California Press, 1983).

4. Carlos Alberto Torres, *The Church, Society and Hegemony: A Critical Sociology of Religion in Latin America*, transl. by Richard Young (Westport, Conn. and London: Praeger, 1992).

5. Collier and Collier, *Shaping the Political Arena*. pp. 15–20.

6. See Carlos Alberto Torres, "Argentina." In Philip G. Altbach, ed., *International Higher Education: An Encyclopedia* (New York and London: Garland, 1991), vol. 2, pp. 869–83.

7. International Student Conference by the Coordinating Secretariat of the Nation al Unions of Students on University Reform in Latin America, Leiden, the Netherlands 1959.

8. Gilbert Guevara-Niebla, *El Saber y el Poder* (Culiacán, Sinaloa: Universidade de Sinaloa, 1986).

9. Raúl Atria, Eduardo Acuña, et al., "El Estado de la Investigación Tipológica Acerca de la Universidad en América Latina." In *La Universidad Latinoamericana: Enfoques Tipológicos*, p. 31.

10. José Joaquín Brunner," Invessgación Científica y Educación Superior en América Latina" (Santiago de Chile: FLACSO, Documento de Trabajo 452, June 1990), p. 2. Brunner qualifies this observation in another work in which he indicates that because of the state's role as financer, the investment in development and research from 1970 to 1980 went from $500 million to $3,500. See J. J. Brunner, "Higher Education and the Formation of the Professional in Latin America" (Santiago de Chile: FLACSO, Documento de Trabajo 380, August, 1988), p. 15.

11. In the writing of this section the following monoraphs by José Joaquín Brunner have been particularly useful: "La Educación Superior y la Formación Professional en América Latina" (Santiago de Chile: FLACSO, Documento de Trabajo

23. James Petras and Morris Morely, *U.S. Hegemony Under Siege: Class, Politics and Development in Latin America* (London and New York: Verso, 1990).

24. Collier and Collier, *Shaping the Political Arena*, pp. 772–74.

25. Sergio Bitar, "Neo-Liberalism versus Neo-Structuralism in Latin American" (*CEPAL Review* 34, April 1988, pp. 45–62).

26. Sylvain Lourié, "Impact of Recession and Adjustment on Education" (paper submitted to roundtable discussion on Development: The Human Dimension, Salzburg, September 7–9, 1986), Fernando Reimers, "The Impact of the Debt Crisis on Education in Latin America: Implications for Educational Planning" (*Prospects*, vol. 20, n. 4, 1990, pp. 539–54); Fernando Reimers, "Deuda Externa y Desarrollo: Implications para el Financiamiento de la Educación en América Latina" (*Revista Brasileira de Estudos Pedagógicos* vol. 71, n. 169, 1990, pp. 195–277).

27. See World Bank.

28. See Juan Prawda, "Educational Decentralization in Latin America, Lessons Learned" (Washington: Human Resources Division, Technical Department, Latin American and the Caribbean, the World Bank, December 15, 1991, mimeograph).

29. Moacir Gadotti, *Convite a Leitura de Paulo Freire* (São Paulo: Editora Scipione, 1989); Carlos Alberto Torres, *Consciéncia e História: A Prática Educativa de Paulo Freire* (São Paulo: Loyola, 1979); Carlos Alberto Torres, *Leitura Crítica de Paulo Freire* (São Paulo: Loyola, 1981).

30. Joseph Maier and Richard W. Weatherhead, *The Latin American University*, pp. 11–12.

31. Maier and Weatherhead, p. 12.

32. See James Petras and Morris Morley, *U.S. Hegemony*, pp. 147–56.

33. In Petras's terminology, this distinction can be applied to intellectuals in Latin America. He reserves the term *lumpen intellectuals* for neoconservative intellectuals who played roles as policy advisors in the Reagan administration.

34. Petras and Morley, p. 151.

35. Petras and Morley, p. 147.

36. Petras and Morley, p. 155.

37. Petras and Morley, p. 156.

38. See a more sophisticated discussion of the implications of postmodernism and post-Marxism in popular culture and intellectuals in Raymond Morrow, "Post-Marxism, Postmodernism and Popular Education in Latin America" (*New Education*, vol. 12, n. 2, 1990, pp. 47–57).

39. See "Twenty Years After *Pedagogy of the Oppressed.* Paulo Freire in Conversation with Carlos Alberto Torres." In Peter McLaren and Colin Lankshear, eds., *Conscientization and Oppression* (London: Routledge, forthcoming).

40. Miguel Escobar, Alfredo L. Fernández, and Gilberto Guevara-Niebla with Paulo Freire *Paulo Freire on Higher Education: A Dialogue at the National University of Mexico*, 127.

41. See Freire, "Twenty Years After *Pedagogy of the Oppressed.*

42. See Carlos Alberto Torres, *Entrevistas con Paulo Freire* (Mexico: Gernika, 1978).

43. Conversation with Carlos Alberto Torres, São Paulo, April, 1992.

44. Miguel Escobar, Alfredo L. Fernández, and Gilberto Guevara-Niebla with Paulo Freire *Paulo Freire on Higher Education*, 131.

45. Miguel Escobar, Alfredo L. Fernández, and Gilberto Guevara-Niebla with Paulo Freire *Paulo Freire on Higher Education*, 123.

46. Miguel Escobar, Alfredo L. Fernández, and Gilberto Guevara-Niebla with Paulo Freire *Paulo Freire on Higher Education*, 143.

47. Miguel Escobar, Alfredo L. Fernández, and Gilberto Guevara-Niebla with Paulo Freire *Paulo Freire on Higher Education*, 149.

2. Curriculum and Social Reality

1. The papers presented at the forum were published in a book entitled *La Nacionalización de la Banca y la Educación Superior* (Foro Universitario, 1983).

2. The process carried out by Dr. Rivero, president of UNAM in the period 1980–1984.

3. Editor's note: Paulo asked me (A. Fernández) not to reproduce that example of East Germany. Leftist authoritariansim is commonplace in our environment, however, whatever the resources used.

3. The Role of the Intellectuals

1. These are translations of the titles of Freire's works edited in Spanish but they may not exactly correspond to the ones in English.

2. *Basist* refers to a leftist ideological deviation, which holds that the popular classes are the exclusive owners of absolute truth.

Afterword

1. Fernandez, Chapter 2 of this volume, p. 163.

2. Freire, Chapter 2 of t his volume, p. 163.

3. C. Delgado-Gaitan, *Literacy for Empowerment: The Role of Parents in Children's Education* (London: Falmer Press, 1990), 2.

4. R. Dale, Review of *Education and State Formation: The Rise of Educational Systems in England, France, and the U.S.A.*, by Andy Green (*Journal of Education Policy* 6, no. 4, 1991), p. 417.

5. Dale, Review of *Education*, p. 417.

6. M. Cranston, *Freedom: A New Analysis* (London: Longmans, Green and Co., 1953); G. MacCallum, "Negative and Positive Freedome" (*Pholosophical Review* 76, 1976, pp. 312–34); J. Feinberg, *Social Philosophy* (Englewood Cliffs, N.J.: Prentice Hall, 1973).

7. Feinberg, *Social Philosophy*, p. 11; Cranston, *Freedom*, p. 12.

8. Feinberg, *Social Philosophy*, p. 11.

9. C. Lankshear, "Literacy and Running Your Life: A Nicaraguan Example" (*Language and Education* 5, no. 2, 1991).

10. Cf. K. Levine, "Functional Literacy: Fond Illusions and False Promises" (*Harvard Educational Review* 52, no. 3, 1982), pp. 261–62; K. Levine, *The Social Context of Literacy* (London: RKP, 1986), 46.

11. F. Cardenal and V. Miller, "Nicaragua 1980: The Battle of the ABCs" (*Harvard Educational Review* 51, no. 1, 1981); V. Miller, *Between Struggle and Hope: The Nicaraguan Literacy Crusade* (Boulder: Westview Press, 1985); R. Arnove, *Education and Revolution in Nicaragua* (New York: Praeger Press, 1986).

12. Oficina de Apoyo para la Pequeña Industria, *Nociones de Contabilidad* (Managua, 1989).

13. Lankshear, "Literacy," p. 96.

14. Lankshear, "Literacy," p. 99.

15. Lankshear, "Literacy," p. 102.

16. Lankshear, "Literacy," p. 103.

17. Lankshear, "Literacy," p. 103.

18. Lankshear, "Literacy," p. 100.

19. Lankshear, "Literacy," p. 108.

20. A. Luke, Keynote address to A Working Conference on Critical Literacy (Griffith University, Brisbane, July 1992); A. Luke, Keynote Address to Australian Council for Adult Literacy Annual Conference (University of Sydney, Sydney, October 1992); A. Luke and C. Walton, "Teaching and Assessing Critical Reading," in T. Husen and T. Postlethwait, eds. (London: Pergamon Press, 1993). See also N. Fairclough, *Language and Power* (London: Longmans, 1989); N. Fairclough, ed., *Critical Language Awareness* (London: Longmans, 1991); N. Fairclough, *Discourse and Social Change* (Cambridge: Polity Press, 1992); J. Gee, *Social Linguistics and Literacies: Ideology in Discourses* (London, Falmer Press, 1990); J. Gee, "What Is Literacy?" in K. Weiler and C. Mitchell, ed., *Rewriting Literacy* (New York: Bergin and Garvey, 1991, pp. 1–11).

21. Guevara, Chapter 1 of this volume.

22. Freire, Chapter 1 of this volume.